Sir Gawayne and the Green Knight

"Though faiths pass, though the philosophies of the great become the shuttlecock of little schoolmen, beauty doth reign ever with her old benignity . . . Do thou but trap her in one tiny ditty, the world in after years shall relearn thy language but to sing it once again."

ARTHUR MAQUARIS (*The Days of the Magnificent*).

SIR GAWAYNE

AND THE

GREEN KNIGHT

A Fourteenth-Century Poem
done into Modern English

by

KENNETH HARE

With an introduction, notes
and a bibliography by

R. M. WILSON

M.A., Lecturer of the Department
of English Language at the
University of Sheffield

EYRE & SPOTTISWOODE

LONDON

First Edition The Shakespeare Head Press
Stratford-upon-Avon
MCMXVIII

Second Edition Eyre & Spottiswoode
London
MCMXLVIII

This book is printed in Great Britain by T. & A. Constable
Ltd., Printers to the University of Edinburgh, for Eyre &
Spottiswoode Ltd., Publishers, 14–16 Bedford Street, Strand,
London, W.C.2

AD COMPTON MACKENZIE

apud quem in insula Jettone poeta amoenissimo hospitio
est delectatus.

Tu Musis grate, erudite amice,
Hippocrenes Tibridisque flavi,
(Et nostri Londiniensis amnis
Cygno dilectique hirundinique)
Fabellarum et conditor facete
Salsarum, qui scribis et dolenda,
Promissum servo—cape hos labores—
Pridem factum : do tibi libellum.
In mentem venit marina gemma
Jetto, comes et tui penates ;
Jetto cujus rubra saxa frangunt
Canentes fluctus.   Canunt alaudae.
Surrident Jettone Pax Ceresque.
Hic narcissi primulaeque veris
Florent.   Hic credam libidinosis
Nautis, nymphas pectitos capillos
Ventis quassos, floribus decoros,
Ostentare et candidas papillas ;
Nautas fallunt perfidae sorores.
Laudo Jettonem insulam venustam,
Libros, auctorem, hospitalitatem.

K. H.

INTRODUCTION

Sir Gawayne and the Green Knight is preserved in the British Museum MS. Cotton Nero A. x, written some time round about the year 1400, and containing three other poems, *Pearl*, *Patience*, and *Cleanness* (or *Purity*), which are generally agreed to be by the author of *Sir Gawayne*. At some time or another this manuscript has been bound together with another containing a panegyrical oration on a certain John Chedworth, a fifteenth-century deacon of Lincoln. The four poems are accompanied by a dozen illustrations in colour, many of them now somewhat indistinct, of which four deal with scenes from *Sir Gawayne*. In all probability the poems were composed some time during the second half of the fourteenth century, and such attempts as have been made to fix the date more closely have met with little success. Nor is it possible to localize them with any degree of accuracy. The history of the manuscript tells us little since nothing is known of it before the early seventeenth century. At that time it appears to have been in the library of Henry Saville of Bank, whence no doubt it passed into the hands of Sir Robert Cotton and so to the British Museum. Its appearance in the West Riding during the early seventeenth century suggests that it may previously have been in the possession of some family or monastic house in that part of the country, but other evidence for this is lacking. Some information on the subject is afforded by the dialect in which the poems are written. As they have survived they are certainly in a north-west midland dialect, but one which was near enough to the northern dialectal area for a considerable admixture of northern forms to be possible. This, however, can only tell us the dialect used by the latest copyist, not necessarily that in which the originals were written. Something of this can be learned from a consideration of the forms used in rhymes—where alterations by a later copyist can often be detected and the original forms reconstructed—and from some of the peculiarities of the alliteration. Such evidence suggests that the dialect of the author did not differ materially from that of the latest copyist, and consequently he might have lived anywhere within a region including South Lancashire, Cheshire, North Derbyshire, or the West Riding. Attempts have been made, by the use of the available linguistic evidence, to restrict this area still further, and different answers have been obtained. In general, however, our knowledge of the smaller divisions of the Middle English dialects is much too slight for such attempts to have much value—a point that is emphasized by the different, and mutually exclusive, results which have been arrived at by different scholars. The only other evidence on the subject is afforded by the description of Gawayne's journey in search of the Green Chapel, since it is only described in detail when the hero passes from North Wales into Wirral. Most of the places mentioned cannot now be identified with any certainty, but the circumstantial detail does suggest a considerable amount of local knowledge on the part of the author. This would tend to place him somewhere in Cheshire or South Lancashire, and various linguistic details have led most scholars to suggest that the latter of these is the more probable.

So far as the author is concerned we know nothing whatever about him, not even his name having been preserved—a fact that has naturally encouraged a good deal of speculation on the subject. The only hint of any name in the manuscript is the fact that a fifteenth-century scribe has written "Hugo de   " in a blank space at the head of *Sir Gawayne*. This may be a later scribe's guess at the name of the author, it may be the name of the copyist, or not improbably of someone quite unconnected with the poems. However, along with other indications, it has led to the ascription of them to the mysterious Huchown of the Awle Ryale, said by Wyntoun, a fifteenth-century Scottish chronicler, to have written on the "Awntyr of Gawane." There is little evidence available to check the accuracy of Wyntoun's statement, and, even if accurate, nothing to show that it refers to this particular poem rather than to another of the numerous Middle English romances celebrating the prowess of Gawayne. One of the works which Wyntoun ascribes to Huchown, the "Pistil of Suet Susane," still survives, and it seems certain that the author of this could have had nothing to do with our romance. Other names that have been suggested have still less to recommend them: the "philosophical Strode" to whom Chaucer dedicated his *Troilus and Criseyde*, one of the Earl of Pembroke's clerks (perhaps John Donne or

John Prat), and John of Erghome, thought to be the author of the *Prophecy of John of Bridlington*. In no case is there the slightest evidence for such an ascription, but unfortunately lack of evidence has not prevented the elaboration of theories. The four poems have been carefully examined for possible auto-biographical references, and on the basis of them hypothetical biographies of the author have been written. If something of his life were known to us from other sources then it might be possible to discover autobiographical references in his works, but when the biography must be constructed from references which may or may not be autobiographical the method becomes absurd. Despite the time and labour spent on the subject all that we can say concerning the author of *Sir Gawayne* is that he lived during the second half of the fourteenth century, that he almost certainly wrote the three other works contained in the same manuscript, and that he may also be the author of a poem on *St. Erkenwald*.

The various sources of the plot of *Sir Gawayne* are fairly well known. Technically we can say that the story is to be divided into two parts, the Beheading Game, and the Temptation or Chastity Test, and that these two parts are joined by the device of the Exchange of Winnings. All three themes are common enough in medieval story, though nowhere else are they found united as here. The first of them, the Beheading Game, ultimately derives from the story of *The Champion's Bargain* in the Irish *Fled Bricrend*, or *Bricriu's Feast*, a work which may have been composed as early as the ninth century. It became a favourite theme in medieval romance, not infrequently with Gawayne as the hero, as in the German *Diu Krône* and the French *La Mule sanz Frain* and *Hunbaut*; elsewhere we find it connected with Lancelot in the French prose *Perceval*, and with Carados, another nephew of Arthur, in the continuation of the *Conte del Graal* of Chrestien de Troyes. The second, the Temptation or Chastity Test, is the subject of Gawayne's adventures at the castle of the Green Knight, and, although the connexion of the various analogues with the version in *Sir Gawayne* is much less close than is the case with the Beheading Game, yet the general theme is found not infrequently in medieval romance, and again quite often with Gawayne as the hero. So, for example, in the Middle English *The Carle of Carlile* and less closely in the two French romances *Le Chevalier à l'Épée* and *Hunbaut*. The device of the Exchange of Winnings by which the two themes are joined appears in no other analogue and may have been invented by the author himself, or more probably adapted from some fabliau, solely for this purpose.

Thanks to the work of various scholars the history of the different constituents of the plot is fairly well known, but when or by whom the three separate themes were all combined into the plot of *Sir Gawayne* are questions which cannot be answered with any certainty. It is unlikely that the combined story is of any great age, otherwise we should expect to find versions of it in earlier medieval literature. The usual theory appears to be that the English romance is a translation from the French, and that it was the unknown French author who first combined the three themes. There is, however, little evidence for any such hypothetical French original, and although the author on occasion certainly writes as if disclaiming all pretensions to originality, it is likely that the phrases are merely the usual medieval conventional appeal to authority and were neither expected nor desired to be taken literally. In at least one case— the account of Gawayne's journey to the castle of the Green Knight—he appeals to "the book" as authority for a circumstantial description which can only be due to himself alone. The author was certainly well acquainted with French romance, but that, of itself, is no reason for making him a mere translator. The usual argument seems to be that *Sir Gawayne* is so incomparably superior to any other Middle English romance that the only possible explanation for this must be a close following of some French original now lost, though as far as that goes it is equally superior to most of the extant French romances.

The hero of the romance is one of the most interesting of all the knights of the Round Table, and certainly in England he appears to have been by far the most popular. Of all the knights only Lancelot has, in Middle English, more than a single romance telling of his deeds, and he has but two, whilst a whole group of romances celebrate the adventures of Gawayne. Originally he appears to have been the hero of a cycle of adventures independent of Arthurian romance and quite as old. But at a very early date this cycle seems to have been absorbed by the growing fame of Arthur, and already in early Welsh legend, in the *Triads* and in the *Mabinogion*, Gawayne is one of the most prominent of Arthur's knights. In Geoffrey of Monmouth, under the name of Walgainus, he is the bravest champion and the most famous of all Arthur's followers in his numerous wars. Already in the early twelfth century his fame had become so widespread that William of Malmesbury thought it worth his while to record the recent discovery of his tomb at Ross in Pembrokeshire. In the early French and German Grail romances Gawayne is almost as important as the hero, and in at least one of them it is Gawayne himself who achieves the quest. In all these stories he is depicted as the ideal knight, unconquered in battle and the perfection of knightly chivalry. But in later French romance no other knight undergoes so marked a transformation of character. The appearance of Lancelot, and his popularity as the chief exponent of the theories of courtly love, brought him into immediate conflict with Gawayne. There was not room at Arthur's court for two such knights, both the personification of all knightly virtues, whilst the purity of Gawayne was a standing rebuke to the adulterous intrigues of Lancelot and Guinevere. Consequently the increasing popularity of Lancelot leads to the degradation of Gawayne's character. He becomes false, adulterous, "light in life and light in death," and even loses his physical superiority, so that Tennyson, deriving his idea of Gawayne from Malory, can describe him as "a reckless and irreverent knight." Such a conception of Gawayne is peculiar to later French romance; in English, apart from a single romance based on French sources in which his character wavers between the two conceptions, Gawayne is invariably the invincible knight, the flower of knightly courtesy and chivalry, "ever doing more than he agreed and giving more than he promised." Not before the time of Malory does the other conception appear clearly in English, and then only in romances based closely on French originals. His popularity lasted long, but as time went on he gradually lost his fabulous character. Holinshed regarded him simply as "a faithfull gentleman, (who) regarding more his honour and loiall truth than neerenesse of bloud and coosenage, chose rather to fight in the quarrell of his liege king and louing maister, than to take part with his naturall brother in an vniust cause." Finally, in a late chap-book, he is represented as living "towards the latter end of the reign of Henry VIII," being described as "a man of some fortune and considerable curiosity, fond of enterprise, and insatiable of knowledge, who travelled through the northern counties of England," his adventures being "extant among the family writings and still recorded by his posterity," a strange transformation for a hero who originally rode a magic horse, wielded a magic sword, increased in strength until noon and thereafter decreased steadily until dark.

The character of Gawayne, as depicted by the author, is one of the great attractions of the romance, but there is very much more in it to delight the modern reader. Critics have been unanimous in describing *Sir Gawayne and the Green Knight* as the best of all Middle English romances, and the reasons for this are not far to seek. One of the qualities which most surely attracts the modern reader is the constructive skill of the author. The rambling formlessness of so much contemporary French romance and the disjointed jerkiness of the Middle English examples are both absent here. The story proceeds from beginning to end with much variety but little digression, and the elaborate descriptions, the arming of Gawayne, the architecture of the castle, the cutting up of the deer, are all kept firmly in their places and not allowed to overshadow the plot. More especially in the third part is this skill in construction evident. The three hunts and the three tests are managed so skilfully and with such variety that there is no effect of repetition. The hunting scenes are contrasted with the tests and the Christmas revels, and elementary though the contrast may be such symmetry is all too rare in medieval literature. Reduced to its essentials the plot is absurd enough, but the fantastic elements are heightened to a grotesque sublimity and despite ourselves we share Gawayne's apprehensions in the final scene. The moral element is always there—both themes are simply tests of knightly honour—but it is never unduly obtruded; the delicacy with which the chastity tests are handled is in striking contrast with the usual medieval treatment, and the way in which Gawayne finally falls short of his own high ideals makes him more human and more likeable. Moreover, the arming of Gawayne shows how the author can handle allegory without letting it run away with him in a way that is all too frequent in medieval literature. One of the greatest charms of the romance lies in the author's use of description; his keen eye, vivid imagination, and use of significant detail, produce unequalled pictures. The dramatic scene at the opening of the poem, the hunts, the scenes in the castle, are examples in which the common conventionalities of the usual romance writer find little place. This is more especially the case with the various nature descriptions, which are far removed from the usual Middle English treatment. Here the author is attracted by the wilder aspects of nature and by the winter landscapes so dear to the Old English elegies. Note more especially the description of Gawayne's journey and the scenery at the Green Chapel, the bitter cold of winter, the icy rain, and mist-covered hills.

Probably the chief attraction of the poem lies in the close intermixture of French and English elements. First of all in the form; the stanzas, of unequal length, are mainly written in alliterative verse directly descended from the Old English metre. Each of these ends with a short one-stress line and a quatrain of three-stress lines rhyming *ababa*. Rhyme and alliteration combine to form a flexible stanza form which only occasionally demands the alliterative and rhyming tags so necessary to the usual medieval versifier. A similar intermixture of elements is to be found in the matter. As a rule French aristocratic romance is concerned with the niceties of courtly love, sentiment is at a premium action at a discount. The English romances are usually written for a lower-class audience which above all prefers action and adventure. Even when the English author is writing for an aristocratic audience the love theme is usually bungled simply because of his unfamiliarity with its conventions. The author of *Sir Gawayne* gives us a straightforward story of adventure, but interwoven, in such a way as never unduly to hold up the story, are the courtly descriptions and love scenes so dear to French romance. It is evidently the work of a well-educated man, accustomed to move in aristocratic circles and writing for an aristocratic audience. As well as any of his predecessors he realized the strength of the alliterative line in scenes of violence, but he succeeded in adapting it to descriptions of the gentler side of life in a way which few writers of alliterative poetry can equal. Especially noticeable is the easy flow of conversation within the framework of the stanza, the subtle use of the two forms of address in Gawayne's interviews with the lady, and the occasional touch of humour as in Gawayne's reply to the taunt of the Green Knight. Both French and English romance must have been well known to the author, and he has succeeded in combining the best from both literatures whilst avoiding their individual weaknesses.

But if *Sir Gawayne* is the best of all Middle English romances it is equally certainly one of the most difficult, and both reasons have led to the appearance of a number of modernizations. If a literal translation be desired prose is the only possible medium, but so much of the original must inevitably be lost in prose that, following Mr. Hare's lead, most translators have turned it into verse of one kind or another. It is hopeless to attempt to keep anything like the medieval form. Alliteration as the sole ornament of poetry has so long fallen into disuse that a modern alliterative poem gives an impression of strangeness and archaism which would not have been present for contemporary readers. Moreover, the demands of the alliteration tempt the translator to retain words from the original which have either been lost in modern English or have considerably changed their meaning. The result is a language which is an unhappy compromise between Middle English and modern English, one that is far too frequently used in the translation of alliterative poetry. It is a type of translation which suggests to the modern reader a roughness and uncouthness quite alien to most of the alliterative poetry. Mr. Hare has avoided this pitfall, and his choice of rhymed verse is certainly preferable. It necessitates, of course, a very free translation; that is inevitable if good poetry is not to be turned into bad verse. The demands of rhyme occasionally lead to the use of a word in a strained sense, or to the employment of an empty phrase, but not more frequently than do the demands of alliteration in the original. Mr. Hare's knowledge of the language of *Sir Gawayne*, his enthusiasm and his skill, have allowed him to retain the spirit of his original in a different metre, and he has succeeded in the *tour de force* of rendering it brilliantly into modern English.

R. M. WILSON,
The University, Sheffield.

SIR GAWAYNE AND THE GREEN KNIGHT

BOOK I

*Of the fashion of King Arthur's Court at Camelot, and of his banquet
made by him upon Yuletide; and of the coming of a Fearsome
Master which laid a challenge that Gawayne took up.*

When siege and battle-shock had broken Troy.
And burnt that burg to brands and ashes grey,
When he that was for guile without alloy
Unmatchable on earth did forfeit pay,
—Tried and condemned by those he did betray;—
Aeneas then, a captain of the best,
Loosed fluttering sails upon the water-way
With his high kith, and sea-tossed won in quest
New realms and golden islands scattered by the west.

Then journeys Romulus with speed to Rome,
Building her white towers with a little band,
When with much boasting thither did he come,
And cast his anchors in the stranger strand,
And named that Rome was erewhile waste and sand,
From Piedmont eastward Langabarde won ground,
And Ticius' navy rocked by Tuscan strand,
But Brutus northward of the silver sound,
Achieved these flowery meads, the fair delightful ground.

A land of war, wreck, wonder, bale and bliss,
And of bold men that loved debate and wrought
Such marvels as from that time unto this
No land can equal. Of Arthur who is thought
Their courtliest King of all, I shall report
The most outrageous wonder ever known
If ye will listen—it is no thing of naught
But from long years recorded and writ down,
And I shall tell it as I heard it sung in town.

THE HISTORY

Arthur the King holds court at Camelot
Upon a Christmastide; his princes there
Were from their many realms together got
To hold rich revel that is the flout of care.
Quick as the nimble creatures of the air,
They met in medley of the tournament
Ofttimes, beneath the fluttering banners rare,
And thronged back thence to Court, the long day spent,
Sworn brothers all alike to newer merriment.

For this same feast was holden fifteen days
Continuously, with all man could devise
Of meat and mirth, with gladsome glee always
Most glorious for to hear; by day they arise
To sportive strains, nor do they close their eyes
By night, but in the dance they mix anon
Lady with lord; thus dwell they, in such wise;
Ladies that lovelier lived there never none,
With knights of most renown excepting Christ alone.

With all the joy in life they met together,
Each with the lady to himself most dear,
Caught by that Christmastide into one tether.
Comely was Arthur, King, by dais there,
And of all ladies loveliest, Guinevere.
Arthur was lofty of spirit, brave in fight;
His men attend by the dais this New Year
His progress, brought to hall with many a knight;
And now the sewers bear aloft the silver bright,

(As clerks make end their chanting of the Mass)
And set the dishes in a double share
To all the knights beside the King's high place.
Loud rose their cries, these clerks and others there,
Who name in drinking, "Christmas," and "New Year,"
And some hold gifts behind them in one hand,
And ask the ladies to debate with care,
And choose; these laugh to be with guile outplann'd,
But laugh the more to have them you may understand.

16

This mirth they make ere yet the meat is brought,
Then wash, and all to supper take their way;
The higher marshalled, as was fitliest thought,
By higher seats; i' th' midst, in royal array
Of thin-spun silk, sits Guinevere the gay
At the rich dais, beneath a canopy
That doth the tapis-work of Tars display
With fair Toulouse, enwoven joyously
With gems of price, with pennies should you think to buy.

She was the loveliest lady to descry
With her grey eyes on any summer day,
(Who boasts a fairer to have seen with eye
Speaketh, but speaketh false, I dare well lay).
Now Arthur might not eat, I have heard say
He loathed long sitting, restless as a child
In all its jolly madness, and as gay
In life's delight, his brain and young blood wild
Keep him from resting, and as yet unreconciled,

Old custom stays his hand from dish and cup,
To drink the red wine or the nappy ale,
Till some newcomer break the matter up
Of an adventurous chance the marvellous tale,
(Yet such as with the credence might prevail
Of the wise men, to be not held a lie,)
Of princes and their arms and silver mail
Or kindred matter; lacking history,
A knight must seek his counter and his jeopardy

Set life at hazard of the chanceful lists,
As trustless fortune shall adjudge the game.
This was his custom at the time of mists,
When frosts with winter airs at Yuletide came,
And therefore, though he may not eat for blame,
He talks the trifles that kings talk at feasts.
Agravayne and Gawayne, pillars of fame,
Each side the Queen attending her behests,
With Ywain and with Bawdwin were the chiefest guests.—

Bawdwin the bishop, Ywain Urien's son;
Agravayne, Gawayne, Arthur's nephews were.
At other boards sits many a princely one.
Then comes the first course with loud trumpets' blare,
(Those golden reeds which painted banners bear)
The noble pipes, the little kettles sound,
Wild warbles wakening startle the clear air
Till the heart leaps for joy, and all around,
Grave seneschals direct bright platters overground

So plenteously 'twere hard to set arights
One silver dish the more, clean upon cloth,
Fresh food was there, abundance of delights,
To each twain dishes twelve and, nothing loth,
Goblets of beer and of the bright wine both,
Now you have guessed (wherefore of this no more)
That staring Want but little business doth
In this bright dwelling, but, the first course o'er,
Came more sounds than clear music as at the great door

A Fearsome Master entering stays the mirth;
From neck to loins most stoutly built of brawn,
Mayhap he was the greatest of the earth
For giant-like so rode he oft by lawn,
Great-backed, great-breasted, though his belt was drawn,
And belly and waist were slenderly beseen;
Unblithe by twilight ere the cocks have crawn
Were he to meet, though fashioned well and clean,
For both his hue and favour were the bright ink green.

Even all was green, this fellow and his weeds,
With a green coat close clinging to his side,
O'er which a peerless mantle brave succeeds,
Lined with bright fur and that displayed for pride,
Likewise his furred hood with the green was dyed,
(Though now caught back, and clasped, and hanging low).
His green hose grip his calves; there might be spied
Striped silken straps beside, with goodly show,
Bracing the bright clean spurs that gleam and greenly glow.

Gay shoes he wore and the rare emerald
Powdered with green stars all his bright array,
His silken stripéd belt the gleam exhaled
Himself, his saddle, and the silk-work gay;
To reckon but half his toys, vain were the essay!
As of his broidery-work of bird and fly:
Green gauds past counting, and amidst them aye
The gleam of cunning gold; the peytrel high
With pendants of that green was glimmering gladsomely!

The stirrups, tail-strap, bridle and saddlebow
Were green or else a-glimmer with green stones,
The steed himself who carries him can show
No hue save green or what with green atones;
His bridle broidered.   That horse was large of bones
For managing by any of a rabble,
But for the present master that he owns,
He found him ever his best horse in stable,
Unto all strange adventures ready and serviceable.

As the steed's mane was green so the knight's hair
Was likewise green, and by the shoulders hung
In wavy locks, and his great beard i' th' air
Seems a green bush when rainy spring is young,
Which beard, and copious hair so thickly sprung
—It was above the elbows trimly cut—
That half his arms were hid his locks among,
And all encircled by his hair about,
Like a King's shoulder cape which closes at the throat.

The mane was kempt and clean and fresh and fine,
And crisped in many a strange fantastic knot;
There was no single hair that did not twine
About a thread of gold that loosened not
Bound all with ribbon, nor had they forgot
The forelock, both were bound and gold-entwined,
And all the tail's length myriad jewels dot
In sparkling eyes, a thong doth all upbind,
With peal of little bells to ring upon the wind.

19

Like the bright lightning in the nether air
It seemed, so they that watched him inly swore—
It seemed that no man mortal anywhere
Might bide his blow and live—yet, strange, he wore
Gorget, nor helm, nor bright shield nevermore,
Nor any plate pertaining unto arms,
But, all red berries, high in hand he bore
A holly-bush that never frost alarms,
Greenest of earth's green things in height of winter harms.

I' th' other hand he bore (what can be liked,
For savagery, to naught that can be told,—
Essay who will) an axe broad-edged and spiked,
—The spike enwrought of green steel and of gold,—
The head an ell-yard long and gleaming cold
Beneath the burnish; shaped shrewd blows to deal,
And sharp's a razor. The huge head keeps its hold
Upon the stock bewound with strands of steel
Inlaid with green, and therebeside looped up with zeal,

And all adown the shaft, and knotted oft,
There runs a thong whence sprightly tassels dance.
Thus moves this knight, but nothing fair nor soft;
Drives to the high-seat, dreading no ill-chance,
Saluteth none, but with a scornful glance—
"Where is," he cries, "the governor of this rout?
I'll reason with him here if he advance!"
He rolls his eyes and glares on all about,
Whilst him of most renown he strives to single out.

A hush falls, all men wondering behold
The green man greener than the grass dew-wet,
Or green enamel upon flaming gold.
Some slightly move, as nearer him to get,
More sit stone-still and utter silence met
His asking, all men gaze with doubtful eye,
Sights they had many seen but one not yet
Wrenched from the world more wondrously awry,
Wherefore the King's word died, the minstrels' melody.

As they were fallen asleep and slumbered all,
They deem these things illusion faery,
And no sound wakens nor no light footfall.
Some, that would speak, withhold through courtesy,
That he to whom they all owe fealty,
May speak before them, wherefore in short space,
Arthur the King makes answer fearlessly;
"Warrior, awhile light down our feast to grace,
Then what thy will is we will learn in time and place."

"Not so by Him that sitteth upon Height!
To dwell here any while is not my will,
But sith the praise is gone forth of thy might
That men esteem thy burg the noblest still,
Thy men the bravest, riding upon hill
Their fleet steeds, and of skill well prov'n and shown
In knightly games, I thought it not so ill,
—Bethinking me of thy high dealing known
And courtesy—to come here claiming as my own

The right to seek some knight in knightly play,
And for a pledge of peace I bear this bough—
I would no war in weeds of holiday!
I have at home hauberk and helm I trow,
Shield, and sharp spear, and fighting gear enow,
Then grant me fair the game I ask by right,
Seeing that the garb I bear makes softer show;
I seek no harm but come for pastime dight."
And Arthur made reply and said: "Sir Courteous Knight,

If thou crav'st battle seek thy counter here."
"Nay 'tis not battle I seek," he cries agen,
"Among these beardless babes what is to fear?
For were I on an high steed armed, why then
Weak as ye be I think among these men
There's none to match me; hearken then and know
What knight soever, bold of blood and brain,
Dare proffer and have back of me one blow
With this axe—let him keep it, it is heavy enow!

21

And if I bide the first I little reck.
And now if any knight a game would win,
And with this rich axe strike me by the neck,
He need but leap here, have it, and begin,
While I stand stiff as stone this hall within.
(He keeps the axe to boot.)   His respite out,
A day and twelve-month, when next Yule is in,
He must come seek my dwelling with no rout,
There have his counter buffet, let him never doubt."

If still at first were they not stiller now?
No sound at all uprose from any side.
The green knight settles him by saddlebow,
And rolls his red eyes searching far and wide
Whoso should rise, and his lithe fingers tied,
Which twitching in his green beard never cease,
Then coughed and with loud tone of insult cried;
"Are these knights Arthur's that whole realms deprease,
Whereof the rumour runs through many provinces?

What boots your boasting, your high insolence,
Your pride, your wrath, your victories all and each,
For now the whole of your renown flies hence,
Sped thither by the words of one man's speech,—
Why, the rogues shake beyond my axe's reach!"
With this he laughed so loud his whole face lined
With wrinkles, but his blushing doth apeach
The King's hot shame, then: "Folly shalt thou find,"
He cries in tones of menace like the rising wind,

"For by Heaven thou dost seek no other thing!
Yet know I none of thy great words afeared,—
The axe, here, and for God's sake!" cries the King
Striding upon him.   The other his bulk upreared,
And vaults to ground, and standing overpeered
By the full head all other in the house,
As with a stern cheer, stroking his great beard,
And drawing down his coat, his head he bows
No more dismayed than if one had brought him to carouse.

Herewith Gawayne from by the Queen's high place
Leans forward crying; "Lo, I thus openly
Beseech my lord to grant me of his grace
To have this play; for if he summon me,
I may approach without discourtesy,
—If my liege-lady think thereof no ill—
For when a challenge is preferred so high
Before your court, though you would have it still,
Yet do these many knights but wait upon your will.

It were unseemly then, as may be guessed,
If all we stir not—none alive more able
Than your knights hereabouts—and I the least
In wit and worth of any of your table,
Shall least be missed; in nothing commendable
Am I, save your blood, Uncle, in my veins—
Then sith this thing is but despicable,
Not worthy your endeavouring, what remains?
Give it me that first asked it, fitter for my pains;

If I speak ill before your knights let them
Determine." Whispering then all judge the same,
To free the wearer of the diadem,
And to Sir Gawayne to decree the game.
So Arthur calls him, and Gawayne ran and came,
And knelt unto him; he lifts him decorously,
Gives him God's blessing and speaks thus free from blame;
"Counsel him, merry Coz, so cunningly
That time enough go by ere he reply to thee!"

Now has Gawayne the axe and should have hacked
Save that the other with an unblanched face,
Stayeth him crying; "Renew we first the pact,—
Deliver me on oath thy name and race,
That I may know thee at the trysting-place."
"Good faith, I Gawayne do this buffet drive,
And then, a day and twelve-month passed in space,
Myself, armed how thou wilt, engage to arrive
At thy house having for company no man alive."

Thereto the Green Knight answer makes again;
"God!" cries the Green Knight, "This delighteth me!
So may I ever thrive as I am fain
To have my blow, thou dost so readily
Rehearse the compact, yet this swear to me;
Swear thou to seek me out upon what strand
Thou dream'st me living, there t' have pay and fee."—
"Thy name nor place I neither understand,
Warrior, where thou dwellest nor in what strange land.

By him that wrought me, speak, where lies thy shore,
Lest wandering I lose thee gone astray,
Whom yet I swear to seek!" He cries: "No more!
One oath sufficeth on a New Year day.
If I shall tell thee, having had my pay,
Where lie my lands, set forth and nothing doubt,
But if I speak not, then the other way,
Thou without blame may'st tarry with this rout,
And live long in thy land and never wend thereout.

Take thy grim tool, let see thy striking now!"
"Gladly," cries Gawayne, making ready boun,
And plants his feet.   The other lowers his brow
And bares his neck, as forward over his crown,
He strokes his green locks that they fall adown;
Then Gawayne gathers the great axe upon height
And sheared through flesh and fat: from his neck-bone,
The fair head fell to the earth, and in despite,
Many start forth to spurn and kick it from their sight.

(The axe stood buried deep i' th' floor o' th' hall.)
Then o'er the green out-twines the oozing blood,
But that dead body doth not falter nor fall,
But starts forth stiffly where the princes stood,
Groping with one dead hand as it were wood
To find its head, and clutched and caught it fair,
Makes for the horse the near'st way that it could,
Bearing his own head by the bloodied hair,
(As him no mishap ailed all headless though he were)

24

Striketh the stirrup, vaults his horse's back,
Then moves slow round that ugly trunk that bled ...
For matter of disquiet few men lack
As toward the dais he sets the streaming head,
Whose eyes unlocking show bloodshotten, red,
And staring broad; then speak the moving lips:
"That thou be ready, even as thou hast said
In these knights' hearing, lest thy fame eclipse,
Look to it ere away thy day and twelvemonth slips.

To have my stroke against that thou did'st show me
Get thee to the Green Chapel, bring no friend,
The Knight of the Green Chapel many know me.
Thou knowest thy compáct; forget not, wend,
Or be known recreant till thy life shall end."
He wrenched the reins and suddenly both were fled
Through the hall-door but whither no mortal gleaned,
For from their sights he charges with the head,
And ever the flint-fire of the hoofs flies out blood-red.

They marvel where he goes, those mazéd men,
But that can none resolve of all the press.
Naught is but question and surmise.   What then?
They hold this thing a miracle I guess.
Arthur with Gawayne laughs at this strangenéss
But cloaks his wonder, saying to the Queen:
"Dear lady, take this no whit in distress;
Apt, apt it is, this craft that we have seen,
A fitting feasting fellow was this man in green

Who graced our dancing, singing and delight,
And yet a strange one I will not deny.
But now to supper can I take me right,
And with glad heart do all things merrily."
He turns then on Gawayne a glancing eye;
"Up with thine axe that hath so amply mown,
Up with it high upon the tapestry!"
And as the King bade straightway was it done,
There by the truest token it makes true things known

Of strangest happenings; then they throng again
Unto the boards, these gay knights all a rout.
Arthur was brought to place and Sir Gawáyne,
And nimble sewers deftly bear about
To each a double portion without doubt,
And minstrels their sweet airs play delicately,
Till daylight dies that is with mirth drawn out
In many lands.   Yet, Gawayne, look and see
That when thine hour is out there shall no tarrying be.

HERE ENDETH THE FIRST BOOK.

BOOK II

*Of the arraying of Sir Gawayne in his Harness, and of the Banquet
Arthur made him, and of his resigned Departure from amidst
those bewailing Knights; and what fair Harbour he won to upon
Christmas Morn.*

This harbinger had Arthur this New Year
Of wondrous happenings; at the banqueting
He spake but little, yet he longed to hear
High boasting tales of any marvellous thing.
Glad was Gawayne when first the year did spring
But heavy may be, doubt ye not, anon:
Though he that has well drunk may laugh and sing,
Fleet flies a year and fellow yieldeth none;
And first and last accord not, oft, nor jump as one.

And this the wise man knoweth certainly.
So this Yule glideth and this year away,
Each season in his order slipping by;
The first is Lent, it needeth not to say,
With feckless fish the hungry to dismay,
Then the world's weather doth with winter chide,
But not for long: here comes a gentle day
When cold sinks down, and the clouds higher ride,
Which send the warm soft showers, and soon on every side

On the fair plains the little flowers may show,
Both ground and groves then green is all their weed.
Birds busy them to build and sing also
For solace, that the Summer shall succeed
Full daintily by many a bank and mead;
And buds in the rank hedgerows thickly crowd,
From sharpness of the pitiless Winter freed,
To swell and bloom when times have them allowed,
And plenty noble notes are heard in greenwood proud.

27

Then, the season of Summer with soft airs,
And Zephyr breathing light on seed and blade.
The trembling leaves drip dew which kindly rears
The herb, all joyously and unafraid,
His leaves to meet the blissful sun dispread.
Then Harvest maketh ware the stubborn grain
Of Winter nigh and not to be delayed.
His drought sends dust full high over the plain
Flying the earth's fair face, and thereto wake again

Grim and wroth winds that wrestle with the sun.
The leaves light earthward from the linden tree.
The tender and green grass is grey anon;
And then all ripes and rots, and certainly
In many a yesterday the year runs by.
If then is Winter the world asks no sage;
His surety is hung in Heaven high,
The white moon, halting in her pilgrimage,
This biddeth Gawayne mind the hour of his voyáge.

And Arthur holds high revel for his sake,
For love of him upon All Hallows Day,
A noble revel he might not forsake.
Though they were sorrowing he might not stay.
They thought to send him joyously away
With a last feast, these knights and ladies all.
Then he said truly: "Uncle, by my Fay,
You know my chances and this matter all,
I crave leave to depart, it may not else befall.

I must go seek the Green Man," he avowed,
"As God shall speed me." Then these knights were fain
To counsel him, with all that peerage proud,
Sir Doddinaval de Saváge, Ywain,
The Duke of Clarence, and that mighty twain
Sir Bedyver and Bors; in dolorous sort
Stood Lionel, Lancelot, Errik, but in vain,
With many a one of worship at that Court,
As Lucan named The Good, and Mador de la Port.

All sick at heart, for they held Gawayne dear
And deemed that he would surely never more
Draw sword with them; but yet he makes brave cheer,
"Though fates with glory or grieving loom before,
Man can but try them" . . . and the long night wore,
And with the fitful winds of the chill morn
He asks his arms; and divers spread the floor
With tapis-work and thereunto have borne
A gilded heap of harness red as the sunset corn.

He tries the irons, each piece is true and good.
His doublet was of precious silken stuff,
Of Cappadocian leather was the hood;
The furs that lined it they were costly enough.
His steel shoes fitted well and nothing rough.
His legs in lovely greaves and without spot
They case, and add thereto the polaynes tough,
Rubbed clean and knotted fast with many a knot
And strap of gold that from the knees they loosened not.

About his brawny thighs the cuishes cling,
Their quaint fantastic clasps were featly caught,
Resplendently his byrny shines, each ring
Woven upon a proud stuff gaily wrought;
His burnished brace and gloves of plate they brought,
And fixed the gold spurs to his heels with pride.
They bring his surcoat with rich blazoning fraught,
Cowters, and girdle-silk unto his side,
And all his gear to shield him through the world to ride.

Each latchet, loop, and stud with gold is red;
Then harnessed as he is, he hearkens Mass,
At the high altar offered and honouréd;
The service over, from the holy place,
He seeks the King and court with easy pace,
Ladies and lords kiss him at leave-taking,
Press all about, commend him to Christ's grace,
And bring him to begin his journeying;
By this was Gringolet upon the ground pawing,

29

Flaunting it restless in his saddle gay
With plenteous pomp of golden fringes dight
And studs of gold; the bridle every way
Bound up with gold; the peytrel hangings light,
The coverture, the crupper, no less bright
The royal skirts that proud i' th' air are blown,
The saddlebows, all bordered for the knight
With studs o' th' rich red gold, of gold each one,
All glimmers and all glows like to the gleaming sun.

The shining helm he hastily clasps on,
Fast riveted in medley not to fail,
Within stuffed and lined warm; aloft it shone,
And there was hasped to flutter in the gale,
A silken kerchief over the aventayle,
Decked and bestuck with gems that glance alway,
And thereon were the birds of hill and dale
Cunningly needled, as the Popinjay,
And Turtles that sit preening through a summer's day,

And truelove knots that both were deft and fine,
(As many a maid seven winters wrought thereon)
But costlier far men saw his circlet shine,
The brave device of sparkling diamond-stone
That clips his helm.   His shield they brought anon,
Whose ground was gules—he slings it by the bright
Baldrick, over the neck, to hang adown—
And in pure gold the Pentangle was pight
Upon the gules; why this pertains to that true knight,

'Tis in my mind to tell.   Bide little rhyme
While I show forth and speak a curious thing;
Tarry my history as for this time.
This sign was set of Solomon the wise king
Who wrought it first, of Truth a tokening.
It has five points and each point each o'erlaps,
And they all lock as endless as a ring,
And sith its fashion hath nor break nor gaps,
It well accords with him who throughout all ill haps

Was faithful found in five and in fivefold.
Honoured by men whom honour made of note;
A good man known and pure as refined gold,
And therefore may he bear his endless knot,
This gentle and true knight in shield and coat.
Faultless were his five wits and failed him never,
His fingers five they failed him not a groat,
In Christ's five wounds his trust was fixéd ever,
From the five joys in fight he might his thought not sever,

For those the Gracious Queen had of her Child,
And therefrom draws he strength of heart and might.
In his shield's larger half her image mild
Rose lively painted, beautiful in sight.
Thereon he ofttimes gazed in cruel fight.
His fifth five Courtesy as doth befall,
And Generous Dealing open as the light,
And Fellowship, not to diminish or pall,
And Pity, Pity that is sum of virtues all.

Above all other knights these are his own,
Enwoven in his heart and true as steel,
And seam and join and sundering are unknown,
It ends at its beginning fast and leal.
This Pentangle it fits him every deal.
And now he is arrayed at full the gay,
Accoutred princely-wise from head to heel,
He gives those men the glad hour of the day,
"For the last time," he thinks, and rides upon his way.

The sparks fly from the hoofs and he is gone
To drive a voyage there might none be loather;
They speak lamentingly who look thereon
(Of the Round Table soothly every brother),
"Time shall go by ere cometh such another,
His fellow upon earth 'twere far to seek.
Arthur had wrought more warely by God's Mother,
To have sent him not all utterly to wreck,
Unto an elvish man his every bone to break!

31

What King was ever to such counsel pressed,
To send a glorious hero from his side
But for a trifle and a Christmas jest,
And that for arrogance and for mere pride!"
The watchers weep.   He may no more abide.
Through many a wildsome track he fares that day,
Through Britain realm he wendeth far and wide,
Friendless save for his foal as histories say,
And there was none but God to talk with by the way.

Much wandering he nigheth to North Wales.
Upon his left hand lieth open sea,
Anglesea isle and ships that push with sails.
By Holyhead runneth a promontory
Whereby is fording, he full wearily,
Seeks thence an uncouth land, an uncouth road.
Of the Green Knight and Chapel asketh he
Of men of Wirral that the wild waste trod,
They prize good men not highly nor love greatly God.

"They had seen none of no such hue of green,
Chapel nor man."   The knight by passes strange,
And many a toilsome bank, climbs saddest of men,
And weary wilds was he fordoomed to range,
And heights to scale.   His cheer was oft to change,
Ere he might see his chapel far away,
Bereft men's loving sights and garth and grange,
And sharp-stung at each ford by the flying spray,
'Twas strange were there no foe to seek to bar his way,

And that so grisly it behoved him fight.
Marvels a many by each mount appears;
'Twere pain to tell a tithing of the sight.
With serpents fought he somewhat and with bears,
With wolves, wild men, and savage mountaineers,
And snorting ettins of the upper crags.
Had not God strengthened him in thick of fears
He were but dead, yet never the more he lags,
Though the rust rots his harness and his gay garb rags.

But worse than battle is the winter season,
The cold clear water shedding from the clouds
That froze ere it the fallow earth might freeze on,
In hail by night. In naked rocks he shrouds,
His limbs half-frozen into an heap he crowds;
Then streams fall clattering sharp and like flint-stone
Icicles hang.
Then sleeps he and forgets both moon and sun,
Of peril and his pain and plight full hard to run.

On a clear morning by a hillock-side,
To Mary Star of Heaven he makes his moan
To bring him, for 'twas now nigh Christmastide,
Unto some dwelling where, no more alone,
He may find succour and somewhat rest fordone.
Praying he plunges deep in forest old,
And marvellous wild with high oaks over stone.
The hapless birds that the bare branches hold
Were piteously piping then for pain of the cold.

He glides beneath them to a frozen mere
Where the sharp winds cut deeper than a knife.
But most he prayeth that he may somewhere
Come to His service, born of maiden and wife,
To free His world from its long brutish strife,
Some day; crying, "Lady bring me to succeed
Unto some chapel lest I lose my life,
In mere waste wilderness, for this I plead,
And I do pray thereto my Pater and Ave and Creed."

So rides he praying, the knight with yellow hair,
And, "the Rood speed me," cries he in his throat,
He crossed himself but thrice ere he was ware
Of a dwelling on a high lawn in a moat.
Everywhere by the stream's edge were to note
Great trees by the hundred rising in leafless glade,
Over earth's winter-white and frosty coat.
A two-mile compassed park the men had made,
And for a pale a spiked and thick-set palisade.

c   33

He sees the castle through the shining oaks,
And sees with joy and shaketh him from sloth;
"Good harbour grant, beseech ye."   He unlocks
His helmet-hasps and doffs it, little loath
In thanking Jesus and St. Julian both,
For Julian brings to housing, books avouch,
The weary wandering pilgrim where he go'th.
Gringolet feels the gilt spurs deeply encroach
And starts forth and they fortune on the chief approach.

The bridge was high uphaled and gates locked fast,
The walls were white and comely and well arrayed,
They shall not fear for any tempest's blast.
A deep-dug double moat the men had made,
The little ripples upon the water played,
The wall went down i' th' water wondrous deep,
And upward haled an huge height undismayed.
'Twas well-wrought stone to the very corbels steep;
Well-wrought the battlements, sound may the inmates sleep.

'Twas white and fair, not builded in an hour,
And all aloft the battlements between
At even spaces, many a gay watch-tower,
With many a lovely loop looked down full clean;
A nobler barbican was never seen.
The hall full high thereafter meets his eyes,
Full thickly pinnacled over the green,
Then carven capitals he did devise,
And chalk-white chimneys many and of noble size,

On tower-roofs of the glimmering stone well shorn.
The man on Gringolet beholds the sight
Of turrets in the frost-light of the morn,
As they were pared from paper seemed they white.
"Within it were no evil," thinks the knight,
"To linger till the feast-time be away."
The porter comes, a purely pleasant wight,
"Good Sir, crave harbour for me for to-day."
"Ay, by St. Peter," cries he, "and without delay,

For this, the next day, and the days you will."
Therewith he clambers down from the high wall
And comes again, and many throng theretil.
They let the draw-bridge at the gate-house fall
And cross out friendly and kneel down withal
On the cold earth him worthily to greet.
To those at the broad gate aloud they call
To fling all wide; he passes over fleet
And bids them rise.   The many starting to their feet,

Some hold the saddle till he shall be lit,
And some lead Gringolet away to stable,
Others about him press, nor cease a whit
To bring him to the high hall and to table.
His helm and brand stout knaves and serviceable
Bear with his blazoned shield away as now.
They heap more firing then to crack and babble,
And Gawayne greeteth each i' th' red warm glow.
Then from his chamber comes the host and bowing low

To greet and bid him welcome that was come;
"Whatever thing is here your own it is."
"Grammercy, Host, Christ quite ye all and some."
Then, as true friend that bringeth not but bliss,
Stoutly he folds him in his arms to kiss,
Then standing back Gawayne regards him well,
He was of prime of life and huge, I-wis,
His eyes as any fire were fierce and fell,
Bearded he was and free.   There is no more to tell.

A captain for an host of goodly men
He seems, to lead them forth in happy hour.
To serve Sir Gawayne one he setteth then.
His bedchamber was built in a bright bower,
And silken coverlets were in that tower,
And comely cloths and curtains curious,
Swung from gold rings; it looked bright as a flower,
For all was tapestry within that house,
And thither is he brought where men his garments loose,

Despoiling him with mirth of his wet weeds.
They bring gay robes anon, a six or seven,
"That he will choose," the chamberlain then pleads,
And one he chose full seemly and that was given,
Glad with all brightest colours under Heaven,
Full-skirted, glowing; "this man surpasses all,"
Thought they that marked, "he who should doubt it even
I think he were a spirit both prone and dull,
For surely never God made man so beautiful.

And what time in the world he lingers here,
On any stricken field where brave men fight,
'Twere far to seek to look upon his peer."
Thus reasoned they that watched, then brought the knight
To the chimney and a chair and charcoal-light,
And cushions passing rich and hassocks quaint.
They clad him with a mantle nobly bright,
Broidered and furred, he needeth no complaint,
The snowy ermine lacked not, but without restraint

Lined both the hood and gown eke sumptuously.
He warmed him well, then mended was his cheer.
The sewers served him, seemly for to see.
They set him up a table on trestles fair
Beside the settle, and spotless everywhere,
They spread upon the boards a cloth full clean.
The napkin and the salt-dish they were there,
And silver spoons, he washed and without teen
Regards the diverse dishes with their sauces keen,

And sundry fishes brought him in a trice,
Baked in the bread or broiled him on the coal,
Sodden or boiled and flavoured with the spice,
And of the sauce so sly he taketh toll,
For sauce he liked. "Do you bring banquets whole
To each chance stranger?" Thereto laughingly,
"Take now this goodly penance, have thy dole,
And after rise amended," they reply.
The wine runs in his head and pain and sorrow fly.

He speaks with mirth as was his wont long since.
Then courteously, by points of questioning,
They seek to learn the country of that prince,
From whence he comes with his much wandering,
Till chances happily him thither bring.
"Of the Round Table," he answers their request,
"Of Arthur the most courteous noble King."
Loud laughs his host, as doth a man well blest,
That 'tis Gawayne arrives at the time of God's own feast.

"Gawayne is come," each whispereth to each,
"He wields all prowess, praise and fair mannér,
Now shall we hear what riches are in speech,
And blameless terms of noble talking hear.
Of God it comes that he should now draw near
When, blithe that He is born, men sit and sing.
Of courtly custom somewhat shall appear
Well worth the learning, and a gayer thing,
Men say he hath the skill and lore of love-talking."

Now falls black night although the day seemed long.
Then to the Chapel clerks seek out the way,
And with the clear bells peal out Evensong,
And ring them nobly at the death of day.
The host plucks Gawayne's sleeve once more to say;
"Thou com'st the welcomest of men to-night."
Therewith they kiss.   Within the Chapel lay
A little chamber quaintly wrought and bright,
And thence the lady comes to look upon the knight

With all her maids.   Most lovely to be seen
For lustrous skin and for her peerless eyes,
Fairer, he thought, than Guinevere the Queen.
He draws near then to cherish her whom he spies
Perfectly wrought of arms and breast and thighs,
And all things else; she did the left hand hold
Of an old lady wrought upon other wise,
Eager and quick the girl, the lady cold,
This full of warm red blood, the other extreme old.

Her snood sewn with clear pearls the wife's hair fills,
Throat bared, her bright breasts show a little in sight,
White as the youngest snow-drift on the hills.
That other muffles it in veil milk-white
Of many folds, which overcovers quite,
And cloaks her swart chin that it not appeared.
With turrets and toys her black brows had she plight,
Naught save the nose and black brows had she bared,
Her lips and eyes and they were wondrous sour and bleared.

Her buttocks broad, and short, and thick I-wis,—
A lady worthy of worship you will say!
But oh that other delightfuller to kiss!
Now when Sir Gawayne glanced upon that gay,
He craves leave thither and departs away;
He bows low to that ancient lady there,
But to the wife, for ever and for aye,
His knightly services he doth prefer,
And a little hasps her in his arms in kissing her.

"Soothly I am your servant at your will."
They lead him thence, the loathly and the fair,
Unto the hearth, and folk the wine-cup fill,
And mix therein the hot spice rich and rare.
The host in fooling springs into the air,
Directing sport and merriment and play;
He takes his hood off with a flourish, and fair
Stakes it upon a spear: "Win that who may,—
The knave that makes us laugh the most shall bear it away!

And I shall venture with the best," cries he,
"Ere I shall lose my clothes unto my friends!"
With such words he makes merry sportively
To glad Gawayne with games in hall, and spends
The night in jollity till each one wends
With lights to bed, and bids adieu to mirth.
Christmas morn breaks, the day the glad man spends
Greeting with festival the Saviour's birth,
And joy awakes in every dwelling on the earth;

Here not the least; with delicates curious,
And stout men for the feasting-tide arrayed,
And that old ancient wife, highest i' th' house,
Sits with the lord beside her, the book said,
And i' th' midst there was for Gawayne laid
Beside the wife o' th' host; then readily
Sewers bear meats while much men laughed and played,
But save themselves, the twain but little see,
Much comforted and blest in either's company,

So dear their dalliance and their whispered words,
Clean and not bawdy, which was to their praise.
The loud trump with the merry pipe accords,
When with much piping minstrels come their ways,—
The little kettle upon the stroke obeys.
Each minds his matters and they theirs, and fair
They drive the second and the third feast-days,
And now the last o' th' feast-days to appear,
The joy of St. John's feast was gentle for to hear.

But there were guests to go on the grey morn,
These wondrous early woke and drank the wine,
And once more danced they, ere, somewhat forlorn,
At last away unwillingly they twine
O'er the bright frost and in the clear sunshine,
But Gawayne going the good man draws aside:
"Unto the chimney in the chamber of mine,
My thanks that you have sojourned here this tide,
My worth is well the more that you deigned here to abide,

To glad with your bright looks my house and feast."
"For your relief, grammercy, in good faith,
But 'tis my worth by knowing you hath increased,
Not yours by knowledge of me," Sir Gawayne saith,
"And God requite you both by holt and heath."
The lord doth all his pains to keep the knight,
Yet with much speaking loseth he his breath,
"For," cries Gawayne, "I must away forthright."
The other him demandeth why he left the sight

Of Arthur's court—should he not grudge to tell—
Voyaging here so boldly and alone,
Ere of St. John's feast yet was rung the knell,
Ere yet the holidays were passed and gone,
With all their bliss, from country and from town?
"You say but sooth," he answers, "I would find
—Where in the world it lieth, to me unknown,—
A land, and this is running in my mind,
Were the whole realm of Britain given me sealed and signed,

I would change it for that country.   Tell me then
If you have heard thereof, or seen with eye,
In what place is a haunt, *The Chapel Green*,
Held by the *Green Knight*, dwelling there hard by?
There was a compact strucken faithfully,
And, but I win there, I may not go back,
And New Year times the tryst, I will not lie,
And of the New Year do but three days lack,
I had rather see the man to set me upon that track

By God's bright Sun than any earthly good.
I had as lief fall dead as fail!" "Ha!   Marry!
The Chapel?" he cries. "It is but through the wood!
Grieve for your tryst no more, nor wander weary,
Till late i' th' day you shall amongst us tarry:
Rest in your bed at ease; long ere mid-morn,
You shall arrive your opposite to harry.
My guide shall point the tracks—be not forlorn—
'Tis but a scant two-mile by Jesus Mary-born!"

Who then is gladder than Gawayne that tide,
Who seeth his voyage to be nigh achieved?
"My dearest thanks, I will with you abide,
And do your will, my care is all relieved."
Now hath mine host his sorrow from him reaved
And brings the damsels from a neighbour room,
For that would do him joy, as he believed.
Then cries he, brawnily where he doth loom,
"Have you not sworn, Gawayne, to abide here all my doom?"

"Ay," cries Gawayne, the other laughing oft,
And monstrous wildly, cries; "Behold and see,
'Tis but to bide the morrow in thy loft,—
For lo, these three days thou hast watched with me,
Nor may'st thou to the full recovered be
With meat and rest, thy journey scarce at end.
If you will, my wife shall bear you company,
For I, if the morn's weather be my friend,
Will to the woods with dawn the huntingtide to wend."

And this grants Gawayne, bowing courteously.
"Yea," cries the host, "then strike we covenant,—
What quarry in the wild wood falls to me,
That quarry change I, never to recant,
Against what falls to thee or great or scant,
Should'st thou win aught; sweet friend, shall this be so?"
"If I win aught," cries Gawayne, "that I grant.
It likes me well that you should play also."
"Then," cries the lord, "bring us to drink, to drink here, ho!

To drink this pledge, to drink this compact sworn."
The sewers bring the wine-cups and anon,
And laughing loud they drain the last drop borne,
To seal the pledge.   Now day is over and gone.
They linger somewhat after the setting sun
To speak soft words, bereft each other's sight,
And comelily they kiss, and one by one,
Each lady she is gone and every knight,
And every man of all with torches gleaming bright.

> And yet ere the company broke
>   They recorded that covenant oft,
> For the old lord of that folk
>   Could well hold sport aloft.

HERE ENDETH THE SECOND BOOK.

BOOK III

*Of the great cheer that the Lord of the Castle made Sir Gawayne, and the
Lord's hunting of the Fox and the Wild-deer and the Boar: and of
the love for Sir Gawayne of the Lady of the Castle.*

The serving-men set tackle in accord,
And truss the mails and see the girths are tight;
And not the last uprose that castle's lord,
Away to the field ere ever it was light.
They ate a sop so quickly as they might,
Unhasped the kennel doors and called agood.
Out come the sleepy hounds with tails upright
Which huntsmen coupled, right as they well could,
And so with bugle-blast away to the gay green wood.

There were an hundred huntsmen, I heard tell,
That rode unto the chasing of that day.
Thrice do the bugles blare, and fierce and fell,
And all aloud the mighty hounds gan bay.
Up to the heights the beaters take their way
To points assigned; the deer that marked the quest
Made all for the heights, but fruitless their essay
For those the beaters fiercely back repressed,—
Then shouting rings and echo glad in gay forést.

They gave the harts their way, and let unchid
The bucks bear thence their branching antlers wide,
For 'twas their close-time and that lord forbid
To speed one shaft where trod the males with pride;
But for the does they drove them from that side
With, "Hay there! Back there!" from the mountain's brow
To where through airy ways the arrows slide
Sped by the bowmen, who are loosing now
A shaft at every deer that darts beneath the bough.

What! but they bleed and die and shriek and wallow,
Struck by the barbs full broad in every place,
And hurtling in pursuit the fleet hounds follow,
While with high horns the hunt comes on apace—
The cry goes up of huntsmen and the chase—
A cry and clang as though the cliff should burst!
Whilst at the beaters' huts, in little space,
And stream and mountain as was plotted erst,
They strike the few that 'scaped the bowmen at the first.

So learned were the lads that held the vale,
So quick the greyhounds running all so light,
So many deer they left to lie i' th' dale
Wherever eye might glance they met the sight.
That lord, who sees his quarry nothing slight,
Cries with pure joy that might not be withstood
"Abloy! Abloy!" and drives the day to night,
With horses trampling and with blasts full good,
Ever away in bliss by merry lindenwood.

But Gawayne the good knight in gay bed lies,
And closely curtained knows not what befalls,
Though night hath wakened in the eastern skies,
And daylight gleams and glimmers on the walls.
But slumberingly he hears a voice that calls
Softly his name, and feels a wind blow cold,
He plucks the curious curtain where it falls
Heavy to ground with scarlet and with gold—
It was the lady there, the loveliest to behold.

She drew the door to as she entered in,
And bolted it with little fingers white.
Long ponders Gawayne what these matters bin
That draw one, fashioned forth so young and slight,
All disarrayed betwixen day and night,
Long he feigned sleep and never word he spake,
Yet marvelling what that case betoken might.
Then she her soft and stilly way doth take
To the bed-side to watch him till he shall awake,

Crept through the curtains and above him hung
O'er the clear counterpane, and did not stir.
Then thought Gawayne: fairly to speak with tongue
And ask what ill-chance hath befallen her
Wherein she seeks my help, were seemlier.
Therefore he feigns to wake and makes to rise,
Crossing, as men do that an harm defer,
Opens his lids and seems struck with surprise,
But needs to feign no wonder at her merry eyes.

Her cheek and chin they were full sweet, full sweet,
And sweetly blent with lovely red and white:
Her little laughing lips they were right meet:
And thus she spake; "Good Morrow to my knight,
So may one steal on you in your despite!
Lo, you are caught, and captive shall be led!"
(And as she spake that word she laughed outright,)
"Think not but I shall bind you in your bed,
Unless we shape us here a truce," the lady said.

"Good morrow, Lady," cries Gawayne the gay,
"I yield myself your prisoner in this case,
And hold that, by my faith, the better way,
For I am taken, I may not quit this place."
Laughing he spake: "but would you grant him grace
To rise and dress, your captive therewithal
Should in all fealty and in little space,
Present him for the doom that shall befall."
"Nay, Marry!" quoth that sweet, "that shall you least of all.

Lie still and rest, this judgment I ordain,
Else shall I fetter fast both hand and side,
For trust me truly ye are that Gawayne
Esteemed of all men whithersoever you ride.
Your honour, your blithe semblance, are the pride
Of lords and ladies and peoples near and far,
Then with my captive knight I shall abide—
My lord doth harry the hind by cliff and scar,
And this an oaken door shot with an oaken bar.

My Lord's men all are to the hunting gone,
And all men else; my women sleep in bower.
And, sith are none here but we two alone,
And none save them could ever scale our tower,
I would not waste but use this little hour.
All the world sleeps or else it rides afield.
You may constrain me that have lesser power.
What though I struggle? I could at last but yield:
Then, sweet, possess you my warm body, your own to wield."

What shall he say? He says; "'Tis my pure gain
That one so lovely set my worth so high.
Yet in my truer colours see me plain,
I reach to no such reverence, dear, pardy.
Yet by the high God I were fain to try
My strength to serve and no occasion miss,
While changing seasons and the years go by.
To be your servant it were joy and bliss,
And he were witless, Sweet, that understood not this."

"The praise," saith she, "that men to women owe,
I undervalue not nor hold it light,
Trust me I were but little dainty so,
To hold fair courteous dealing in despite,
And gentle words of lady and of knight,
But though I offend a little seeming too bold,
A maid to win you, Dear, to her delight,
To comfort and drive hence her sorrows cold,
Might waive what else of wealth her treasure-houses hold.

I love that knight that is of so great fame
That to the height of Heaven it doth aspire,
The earth is grown too narrow for his name,
And here he lies all wholly at my desire."
But not her favour nor her lovely attire,
Nor cheek nor chin could win him as she would,
He counters speech with speech, but without fire;
"Folly is all men give me by the Rood,
Set beside one bright word of thine that knows but good."

"Oh Mary Mother, but otherwise say I!
For were I worth all women in the land
And wished to make my chaffer thriftily,
Holding the wealth of nations like thin sand,
Or wrought into one jewel to my hand,
Then for all I have heard and count for true,
Here in your chamber would I take my stand
To chaffer, know you not what I should do?
There should no knight on earth be chosen before you."

"I-wis," he said, "there's many a better man,
Yet am I proud so highly to be priced,
And in all faith, in all that ever I can,
I am your servant and requite you Christ."
One thought him potently from love enticed,
The buffet waits to stretch him stark and cold,
She might be fair indeed, but that sufficed.
'Twas now mid-morn and past, then; "Sweet, I am bold
To take my leave," quoth she: he did it not withhold.

She turned to go but with a glancing eye,
"Gawayne the knight it cannot be," said she.
"Wherefore?" he asked and quickly made reply,
Fearing he lacked some point of courtesy,
But she resolved him, saying: "had it been he,
Sure he had kissed her ere his lady passed."
"Lady at her commandment," answered he,
But she upon the sudden, no whit downcast,
Drew near and flung her arms about him and held him fast,

Knelt down and caught and kissed him passing fair . . .
Then each commendeth other to Christ's grace,
Then, without more ado, she left him there.
He hastens him to rise and dress apace,
That blithely and anon he may hear Mass,
Thereafter to the presence to proceed
Of those two dames, and to the dining-place,
And then to dinner and hungrily to feed;
He calls his chamberlain and chooses him his weed.

And welcome did he find, that merry day,
Betwixt the older and the younger dame,
That courtly pair, for still with sport and play
They sped the hour, much solace set those same,
With mirth until the moon rose, and with game.
And still by wooded heath and hillock brown,
Plying his craft, that lord wherever he came,
Enwrought such havoc, they raised to his renown
A pile to wonder at before the sun went down,

Of does and barren hinds and such like deer.
Then fiercely flocked that folk in at the last,
And of the quelled a quarry made them there,
Whereto the best men hied them and full fast,
And first, the fattest upon one pile cast,
In act to undo them, them they overhaul,
And at the essay they searched them, some that passed,
And did aloud unto their fellows call:
"Two fingers thick in fat: the thinnest of them all!"

They slit the hollow above the breastbone then,
And seizing the erber, fast the free ends tied,
They rip me up the limbs with little pain.
And in a trice they rend me off the hide.
To have the bowels, they break the bellies wide,
Then void them forth; anon the knot they raught.
They gripped the gullet, and securely wried
Weasand from windhole; then the guts they sought,
And threw them out, and with their sharp knives off they brought

The shoulders, by a cleft, with unbroke sides;
They break the breast then, riving it in twain;
Back to the gullet then, which one divides—
Right to the bight he rips it up amain,
And voids the avaunters yarely from the slain—
The skirts o' th' ribs thereafter they unlaced,
Right down even to the haunch, which they distrain
And heave it up all whole, when they uncased
And cast the numbles forth, and with like dexterous haste,

47

They lance the flaps behind the fork o' th' thigh,
Then by the spine they hack the same in two;
They cause the neck and trunk asunder fly;
They pierce the flanks which from the chine they hew,
(While one into a copse the crows'-fee threw)
And by the fork's-hough hang them; plenty abounds;
Each takes his fee; then bread with blood they embrue,
Whilst gall, paunch-leathers, lights, someone impounds,
Upon a fell o' th' fair beast to feed their hounds.

Men blow the Prys, and loud they bay, the hounds,
Obtain their flesh, and then all homeward hie,
And many a lusty note that eve abounds,
And blast of horn, and that whole company
Reach their fair castle as the day doth die;
There sits Gawayne full tranquilly in stall,
Anon the lord makes entry merrily,
And by the bright fire kindled in the hall,
He and the gay knight greet, and pleasure comes at call.

With many a careless and trim-coated page,
The ladies soon descend by the broad stair,
With all their maids.   The lord bids clear a stage,
And to bring in from out the frosty air,
And to set down his goodly beasts and fair.
He points to their tails and loud that all may hear,
He cries: "Have I won thanks that spend such care?
All this is thine by covenant full clear."
"I thank you," cries Gawayne, " for not this seven long year,

In winter, have I seen so big a prize!
And this is my gift with the like good-will;
Such things for us at home the times devise,
And we no less our covenants fulfil."
Then is the talking and the laughter still:
"What hath Gawayne, what hath he hid in store?"
"I won this fairly, as by holt and hill
You won your hinds," speaking he crossed the floor,
And kissed the lord full fair, "'tis yours even were it more!"

Then was loud laughter in the tap'stry hall
That every oaken rafter rang of it.
"But," cries the lord, "how did this thing befall,
And how won, say you, was it by your wit?"
"Nay," cries the knight, "I cannot find that writ,
It is not compact, seek no more as yet."
Then to the chimney do they go to sit,
Where at the supper all the house is met,
With rare wines borne in cups and newest dishes set.

And ofttimes in their mirth they make accord
To hold the like compáct the morrow morn;
Gawayne at home and overland the lord,
By field and fold with horse and hunter's horn.
Then the bright liquor is towards them borne
To drink the pledge, "What thing the morn supplies
Of new, to change." And now night comes forlorn;
They greet the unsought sleep with heavy eyes,
And leave the hall to shadows and a fire that dies.

Before the cock has crowed and cackled thrice,
That lord has leapt from bed to quit the place,
Mass o'er, and meat, they are gone thence in a trice,
Ere the first gleam of day, dressed for the chase;
They pass by the high towers the open space
With mickle blowing of the merry horn.
The hounds that through the woods must run their race,
Mighty and fleet, beneath a bush of thorn,
They loose where a great crag shoots up beside the bourne.

The hunt cheer loudly, and the brawling pack,
Forty at once, unto the trail fall straight.
Crag, valley, dale and hill give answer back,
Hounds bay, horns blare, rocks ring, that beast to bate.
There stood, from the steep height fall'n sheer of late,
A mound grown wild with rank copse round about;
Well know the keepers what beast lies in wait,
And while they beat the bushes, all that rout,
Those with the bloodhounds swear that they will have him out!

D   49

Then out he rushed, there is no more to say,
And flung three men to ground, and forth is gone,
A fell wild-boar that, gone is many a day,
Had quit the others to harbour there alone,
—A beast unblithely met by stock or stone—
They sound recheat and after drive pell-mell,
But where he turns there's many a man may groan,
Thrown to the earth, yet they entreat him well,
Riders, horses, and hounds full brave that beast to quell.

Ofttimes he makes a stand with vicious eyes,
Then the wood quakes to hear the hunters' "*Hay!*"
But piteous are to hear the bloodhounds' cries
Torn by that wight so savage and at bay,
Yet when the bowmen draw he dares not stay,
—Though all their strength of arm cuts not his hide,
Which is so rough it sends to splinters grey
Whatever strikes it—yet he starts aside,
And wounds both horse and hound and many a man beside.

For when he felt the shrewd and bitter stroke,
He waxed all mad for battle and debate,
Forth from his jaws the yellow torrent broke,
Then many ran from him that chased him late.
The lord on his light horse but laughed thereat,
And dashes after, and doth his bugle blow
Right through the brushwood where the beast doth bate,
The others follow sith the one dare go,
And chide their fierce wild swine until the sun is low.

This while within Sir Gawayne lies abed,
Yet travel-wearied, but in richest gear.
The lady woke, she kept no sleepy head,
But in his chamber lovely gan appear,
And draws back from his bed the curtains clear.
"I muse," said she, "if you are ever so,
The courteous customs that I teach you, dear,
It seems you do so little care to know
That what you learned yestreen to-day away you throw.

I taught you, though you have forgotten, sweet,
One the most truest token I have known."
"What, for I know not, have I said unmeet?
If you speak sooth, the blame is all my own."
(She sits beside him now, this twain alone)
"What said? 'Las! what not done! I taught you this;
Where a delightsome countenance is shown,
The knight adventurous will claim a kiss,
And this becomes him well, such privilege is his."

"Call back," he says, "my dear, that speech of thine,
For what if he did this and were denied?
Fairly to him she might nowise incline."
"What fears he?" saith she, "having on his side
Strength to constrain with loveliness allied,
Were she so churlish to deny him still."
He says, "Your fair speech, lady, is my pride,
But gifts, men say, the givers' selves do spill,
And gifts are gifts no more, lacking the givers' will.

But, lady, use me ever at your good will,
I am your knight to kiss in any place."
Therewith the lady leans down soft and still,
And very comely kisses his fair face.
Of loves despised and lovers winning grace,
They spake much matter. "I would learn," quoth she,
"Wherefore it falls, would you resolve the case,
That active men and full of courtesy,
And bred unto the trade of arms, men such as ye

In whose works both the title and the text
It is of toils endured for their mistréss,
(They jeopardise their lives in battle vexed
To win her love, and for no matter less;
Or long enduring hardship and distress,
At last avenging her, they cool her care,
And their reward of labour her caress)
But you whose name and fame walk everywhere,
Give not the poorest little word away to bear

Of anything pertaining unto love;
But, if unskilled, how got you such high praise?
Then come I seeking you to learn thereof,
And with you have I sat these two dull days,
But though my lord was far on foreign ways
Chasing his harts, I had no mirth nor game.
Then guide a youngling through this crafty maze,
Or I shall hold, and that were worthy blame,
You hold I am too senseless-dull to learn that same."

"My silence was a thousand leagues away
From thinking so," cries he, "'tis pure delight,
When with whatever cheer thoughtful or gay,
You kill an hour in playing with your knight.
Of love I spake not for it passed my might,
For how by *me* should true-love tales be told
To *you* that in such practice have more sleight
Than I, though an hundred like me were enrolled
To prompt my wit?   That were a folly manifold!

But truly your poor student I would be."
Thus parries that gay knight with quick defence.
To work him woe long time essayeth she,
But no word fit for blame she draweth thence,
For Gawayne was so clean from all offence,
Courteous and noble.   Fairly then ends this.
The Mass bell rings, she must be parted hence,
Or be known absent; once more doth she kiss,
Then leaves her knight full slow and wends her way I-wis.

The lord this while is faren over land,
To drive his swine with blood-hounds by the brae,
Who cruel bites their backs at every stand,
Till low in dirt and trodden mire they lay.
Then come the bowmen driving him away,
Spite of his teeth with thick-sent arrows flying.
Then he takes water, and to bide his bay,
Swims to the mid-stream where a crag is lying,
And gains his den forspent, the echo round him dying.

He sets his back unto the hollow stone,
And scrapes the flints and hideous clamour makes.
He sets aloft his bristles up each one,
Whilst from his jaw the foam in fury breaks
Which the wind catching, tosses thence in flakes.
He whets his tusks, fit monster for a dream,
And all men hold them far for their lives' sakes,—
The lord that God nor devil did esteem
Alone leaps from his horse and wades into the stream.

The silence falls on those beside the brook
Who tremble for his life, watching afar,
They count the moments and dare scarcely look
Upon the water, a diminishing bar.
His flourished brand they saw bright as a star—
Then the boar charged and water o'er them spread,
But he has marked him nobly at that jar,
And through the belly drove it to the head,
The boar went swiftly down the water so well he sped.

Hounds bayed, men shouted and the horns blew clear—
Then an old huntsman, learnéd of long date,
Draws from his belt a sharp knife and a shear,
And rips me up this fellow, dead by fate,
And all this matter shortly to relate,
They lash the feet to a stout pole and strong,
But the huge head with pomp and mickle state,
They mount in triumph to be borne along:
Then with no small content they quit the wood with song!

He thinks time lagging till at twilight-fall,
He sets the boar beneath his roof; he said:—
"Mark well the girth of him, then praise us all,
We woodmen that so thriftily have sped.
We forced this fellow's hold, through the woods he fled,
At rout I slew the great, the big of brawn."
They handle in amaze the heavy head
That in the woods deftly away was shorn,
"A boar the greatest of the world," they will be sworn.

"And flesh and fell, Gawayne, he is your own
By our fast compact faithfully and true."
"I grant it sooth, nor need you give alone,
For I have yet wherewith to change with you."
Then twice he kisses him, thus true men do,
Quit all oaths sworn at fall of eventide.
"St. Giles!" the host cries, "never yet I knew
A better man at chaffer, far and wide,
Men may grow rich apace, the country where you bide!"

Laughing he speaks, the while the boards aloft,
Laid on the trestles and fair covered all,
Await but supper.   Then lights waken soft,
And waxen torches glimmer by the wall,
And mirth and glee ring loud through oaken hall,
And supper done, the minstrels close the day
With Christmas songs and notes that gaily fall,
Nor yet the lady ceased her amorous play,
For where Gawayne was found she was not found away.

But all the time she did so look and glance
Beneath her lashes, that he wondering,
Was inly wroth that so these things should chance,
But though she strives long time to wrest the thing,
He makes her in return no proffering,
Yet lacked no courtesy at first or last.
And now the minstrels play no more nor sing,
And all to the red chimney forth are passed,
Where a new compact for the morn the host has cast.

But Gawayne craves his leave for parting thence,
For that his term is all too nigh at hand.
"Why?" cries the host.   "Is it so far from hence?
And anyone can show thee overland
Where thou may'st end this matter out of hand.
Thou shalt, ere prime, I swear, achieve thy quest.
Our pact is struck, besides, that understand,
And thou art proved true twice," he cries in jest,
"To-morrow is the third time and shall be the best.

54

And I shall hunt afar these frosty woods,
And when we meet with evening in this hall,
We will anew make proffer of our goods,
If with good hap the morning shall befall."
And this grants Gawayne and agrees to all.
"Sith you forbear one day to seek your ill,
Here lie and rest and think of joy withal,
When it is found then take of joy your fill,
For sorrow takes the man at any hour she will."

* * *

The Mass is sung to end, the pages wait
The guests' arrival and upon them pressed
The sops in goblets, while to the main gate
The serving-men bring coursers of the best,
For all that troop is to the hunting dressed;
Brisk is the earth with frost on stock and stone,
And the great steeds impatient of arrest,
And as with joy departed is each one,
Out from his cloud-rack ruddy rose the mighty sun.

When they had ridden to the greenwood side,
The hounds of their long leashes free they cast.
A traverse way athwart the wood they ride,
And through the horns they blow a rousing blast.
A little hound that by a thorn-bush passed,
Shrilly gives tongue, his fellows answer back,
The huntsmen cheer, the rabble fall in fast,
Hounds swift and lithe follow the fox's track,
As forth by many a difficult grove he leads the pack.

He swerves, he backs, he doubles, oft he crept
Beneath some sharp hedge, marking far away,
How fast drew on the hunt, then quick he leapt
Over a spinney, leading them astray,
And scaped the forest, and had won the day,
But that a beater's hut was stationed there,
Wherefrom three fierce ones ran at him all grey.
So to the woods again poor wretch in care,
With all the woe in life and courage of despair.

Then was it very bliss to hear the hounds
When all the pack had view of him together,
Such outcry for his head, as from their bounds
The clambering cliffs had clattered altogether,
No gambler on his life would stake a feather,
Full loud they holloaed when they came at him,
And, "thief! thief!" cried, and in the greenwood tether,
Those tattlers at his tail with eyen grim,
Hem him lest out again he dart from forest dim.

By hollow, by hill, he leads them, over, under,
He misled well that stout lord and his train,
He twists, he twines, lest he be torn asunder,
And far he flies and sly creeps back again. . . .
But within curtains doth the knight remain
All that cold morn asleep so wholesomely;
Not so the lady, thinking upon Gawayne,
Love keeps her waking; stealthily drew she nigh,
Nor suffered her fixed purpose from her heart to fly.

Her merry mantle falls with many a fold,
Furred all with costliest furs so fair and clean,
She wore not on her head the heavy gold,
But well-set jewels, like the stars for sheen,
Clustered by twenties in her locks I ween,
And breast and back she bared for more delight,
And shot the heavy bolt the hasps between,
And flung the lattice wide where day sprang bright,
Then with her merry words she woke the sleeping knight,

"Lo how thou sleep'st upon so clear a day!"
He lay in turmoil of a troublous dream:
No more debate! he taketh the right way,
And how the Chapel all horror doth beteem,
He greets the Green Man, grisly doth he seem,
And stern he bides the buffet at the tryst—
But, as she spake against the morning beam,
He answered, and the lady as she list,
Leans over his fair face and him she featly kissed.

Nobly he welcomes her, and with good cheer,
That was so glorious in so gay attire,
Faultless of feature and of colour clear,
That very bliss doth set him all afire.
Good words they spake, and in glad time aspire
To bliss and playful dealing in accord,
And ever with the hour is danger nigher
Lest in the game the present times afford,
She may forget a-hunting she hath left her lord,

For this fair knight so hotly she beset,
And of her love made show so plenteously,
That either he must pay again the debt,
As very traitor to that hostelry,
Or make denial with foul discourtesy,
Wherefore this tale of hers and fair behest,
And all that tends to love in specialty
He sets aside, as it were done in jest,
"Nay, Sweet," quoth she, "give heed unto my poor request.

Of all men living you have of blame most part,
If you can love not her who lies by you
Above all women wounded to the heart!
Have you some other leman of fairer hue,
With sweeter lips and eyes of lovelier blue,
Holds she your faith so fast, this fairer one,
—For that there is one such I hold it true—"
"Nay," cries the laughing knight, "for by St. John,
I know none, nor as at this time, I would know none."

"That is a word the most unkind of all,
Answered with answers that are ill to hear!
But kiss me once and I take leave withal,
This one time only, nothing is to fear."
And she bent over him and kissed him there.
"I can but mourn as this wide earth I rove,
But at this parting one gift give me, dear,
Though all so little a thing as but thy glove,
By this to think on thee and looking ease my love."

And he made answer, "I were then most glad
Having such gifts as princes have in store,
Samite and sendal would to God I had,
And sprightly jewels, these thou should'st tell o'er
And choose the rarest, worthy still of more,
But, lady loveliest, take it not in pain,
You know me voyaging an unknown shore,
No brave delightful things borne in my train,
And gloves—that were a wretched giving for Gawayne!"

She reached him then a ring, a toy full proud,
Whereon was set a ruby thence to stare,
Like to a sun half-hid in golden cloud,
With dazzling shine melting the shady air.
This did she proffer him with speeches fair,
A thing of value huge in show, pardie,
But yet he granted not her ring to wear,
But makes his answer; "Hostess mine, let be;
I will have naught of you sith you had naught of me."

"If you deny to have my ring," quoth she,
"Lest you a guest should be too highly graced,
And would not thus beholden to me be
For precious things, have this," and she unlaced,
Wrought of green silk, with gold-work well enchased,
Warm with the clinging to her body white,
The slender ribbon from beside her waist,
Broidered with fingers, pleasant to the sight,
This she besought him take and wear and be her knight.

"Have this, though worthless, sith you will no more."
But the knight answered, "Never in no case
Treasure nor gift he might not have before
He met his counter at the trysting-place,
To win his chance, thereto God send him grace."
She urges him, he sets her gift aside,
"But, lady, wear no sorrow in your face,
I am your servant truly and with pride,
Serve you through hot or cold wherever I may ride."

"Do you deny my gift," the lady said,
"For that so simple it appear in show?
Lo, to the sight 'tis but a little thread,
But for its virtue other far than so.
Learn then to judge aright and truly know
Who girds him in this ribbon, from that while,
Under Heaven's height he need not fear a foe,
Nor point, nor edge, nor bloody wounds and vile,
Nor craft nor sleight at all of no enchanter's wile."

Then he accepted it full fair and free,
For casting in his mind it seemed clear gain,
A jewel for the morrow's jeopardy,
"For by this sleight," thought he, "to scape unslain
After long toiling and incessant pain
Were pleasant end." She gave all with good-will,
And prays that none may know it but they twain,
And this her wish he granted to fulfil,
Then the third time she kissed him and went forth full still.

So has she taken leave and left him there,
For more of that man's love she might not win.
Then rose Gawayne and hid the lace with care,
There where he hopes again to find it in
A privy place, and calls his chamberlain,
Who brings his sprightliest weeds against that day;
So to the chapel, and the priest within
Bids shrive and teach him to the better way,
He sets him all as clean as though for Judgement Day.

Then makes he merry with those ladies there,
With dancing and all manner bliss till night;
Never before so joyous was his air,
Not till that hour showed he so gay a sprite;
He jests with all; all mark his pleasant plight;
There leave we him that merry band among,
With love, with ladies, and with all delight:
Whilst hard o'er land, that lord yet heads the throng;
He hath nigh worn out his fox: the shrew he hath followed long!

They met him coming through a full rough grove
With all the rabble right upon his heel.
With whip and spur forward that lord doth shove,
Draws from his scabbard his brand, about doth wheel,
Brandished and flung it: stark doth Reynard reel,
Scaped it, and thought to start back through the crowd,
But fleeter is a hound his death to deal,
All at the horses' feet, thick as a cloud,
They worry me this cunning fellow snarling loud.

Nimbly adown to earth doth that lord light,
And caught and overhead bore high his prey,
Thither the nearer huntsmen speed aright,
To mark the brave hounds all aloud that bay,
Faint the recheat is sounded far away,
Till gathered is that company all whole,
Whose loud hallooing closes up the day,
While all that ever bore bugle blows his dole,
So merry do they raise the Mass for Reynard's soul.

They stroke their gallant hounds and fee them well,
Then turn back home tearing off Reynard's coat,
The purple twilight gathers in the dell,
Their mighty horns they blow with lusty throat
Full stoutly, so they come by ditch and moat,
And find a great fire on the floor agood,
And Gawayne and that company of note;
His blue robes trail to ground right as they should,
Brave is his furred surcoat and nobly hangs his hood.

And he makes answer, saying, all in game,
"Sir Host, fulfil we now our compact right
Which being left undone deserveth blame,
Even that same treaty strucken yesternight
Where lacked no drink," then thrice in all men's sight,
He kisses him so gravely as he may.
"By Christ! a goodly bargain!" cries that wight,
"Gave ye as good for what ye took to-day?"
"Enough," cries Sir Gawayne, "if what I owe I pay."

"Herein," the other cries, "I am behind,
For though we chased agood while we had light,
Save this foul fox-skin nothing could we find,
May the Fiend have the goods and take his flight!
For such a quarry is a thing too slight
To change against three kisses all so good."
Yet had Gawayne the love-lace hid from sight,
And says but thus: "I thank you by the Rood."
Then the whole story of that hunt in joyous mood

They tell him, ere with meat and minstrelsy,
They make them merry at the banqueting,
And drive the sullen time away, perdy,
With ladies' laughter light, with gay jesting,
With wine, with mirth, and many a pleasant thing,
Till servingmen with torches burning bright,
Lighten that host and all to chambers bring,
Then for his sojourn Gawayne thanks that knight;
"The honour due to you may the High King requite,

For me I rest your servant faithfully.
But hearken, Host, I go hence with the morn,
And therefore now a fellow lend to me,
To guide my ways, though wild, to that drear bourne,
Goal of my wanderings all, Chapel forlorn,
To embrace the doom of God ere joyous day
Laugh in her east." "That," said he, "I have sworn,
And evermore in all things else obey,"
And then the fellow he assigns to point the way,

By weald and waste the tracks least intricate;
He shall not toil at crossing of the stream,
Nor at the tangled copse in double abate
His ways, so high that hostel doth esteem
The guests' well-faring; ere the morning-beam
He shall away full early on the road,
And their cold sighing doth them well beseem,
That court and ladies all that there abode,
Who kiss him fairly fain commending him to God.

So has he left them and to each man met,
That with his diverse toils had served him, said
Fair words at parting; torches high are set,
And twinkling tapers lighten him to bed.
That the warm sleep, though kingly canopied,
Bring him to harbour out of billowy thought,
I dare not say; he has within his head,
Matter to muse on in the blow he sought.
Bide yet a little: I will tell you how they wrought.

HERE ENDETH THE THIRD BOOK.

BOOK IV

Some matter of the Host of the Castle and of his Wife that loved Gawayne; and of the Varlet which led Gawayne to the Tryst of the Green Chapel; with the manner of his Encounter with the Green Knight and the End of this Enquest.

By this it was the last watch of the night.
Then at the word of God the morning woke;
And charged the dark and overthrew him quite.
Wild weather in the world with tempest broke;
What shall he now that lacketh shoes and cloak,
When the furred coats of beasts the sleet soaks through?
The driving snow doth stream and valley choke,
And loud about his towers the great winds blew,
And Gawayne lay and hearkened every cock that crew.

His eyes were closed, but little did he sleep.
Then quickly up he rose, where by the wall,
A little lamp kept watch in darkness deep.
His chamberlain awakening to his call,
Bestirs him and, as fitly doth befall,
After a great wise fashions his array;
A crafty garb he meets the cold withal;
His harness-rings, the red rust rubbed away,
Shine like a running brook upon a morn of May.

No freshlier looked Gawayne when first he rode
From Camelot; his plates picked clean each piece.
He calls for Gringolet from his abode,
And from the stables yarely they release
I trow the gayest horse from here to Greece.
The knight himself does on his noblest trim,
To search the velvet out he doth not cease,
And his coat-jewels like a starlight dim,
Shone in the grey of morn and that was well with him.

For should I tell the garments that he wore,
His coat of the proud velvet furred and brave,
Was with the clear stones broidered over and o'er.
Merry and bright the gems and good to have;
For the wrought seams the craftsmen did not save
The broidered curious work, for greater pride,
The underface was furred, and that she gave,
The lady, he forgot not at that tide,
But knit it by his body ere he garbed to ride.

He wore it neither for the red nor green,
Nor for its pendants of the gold full clear,
For its rare grace (the like was never seen)
But only for that life he held full dear,
And would prolong it with a charm to wear,
As any would that loved the stars and sun.
Now Gringolet full restive gan appear;
By this Gawayne his bright brand belted on,
And gives that folk farewell throngs to the stairs of stone.

Then garb they the great Gringolet likewise,
—The proud one would away in air so cold—
Then soberly he spake in seemly guise:
"There is a folk within this castle hold,
That think on honour, may all joy enfold
Them and their lady and lord by night and day,
And by good men it shall be often told,
'They cherished those who wandered by the way,'
And truly if I live somewhat I will repay."

Then with his shoe he strikes the mounting-steel
And strides aloft; his bright shield bravely shone;
He girds at Gringolet with golden heel,
Who at that bidding starts upon the stone;
The bridge is down, the gates full wide are thrown,
The steeds abide no more with hooves to prance,
But ere the knight beyond the pale is gone,
"God give," he cries, "this castle aye good chance!"
So parts he, with the youth who bears his spear and lance.

The porter, kneeling, cries unto the knight,
"Sir Gawayne, God you save!" then from that folk
He and the youth departed are full light,
Beneath the naked boughs of ash and oak.
Beyond their banks the torrents boiled and broke,
And damps and vapours choke the path they tread,
Each mountain had of mist a hat and cloak,
And lonely by the wood that wild way led,
And in the cloudy rack the sun withholds his head,

He doth disdain the hour and will abide.
They breathe their horses on a hill full high,
And mark the desolate snows on every side.
And now the youth, halting his master by,
Bespeaks him; "Here a man can see with eye
The Chapel bounds, but truly in this case,
There is another way, I will not lie,
Work by my wit, and if God grant us grace,
We may yet fly full fleet and scape this perilous place.

Though I offend, I say it but for love,
I would not meet the ruler of this waste
For anything on earth, by God above!
That giant of this middle earth, encased
In his stiff irons, is no man to be faced
By any four knights of King Arthur's court.
See, here beyond the dale his home is placed,
And he is pitiless, from that resort
There's neither monk nor mass-priest bringeth us report,

Chaplain nor churl nor any living wight.
He slayeth all alike by the hard hand,
And for that butchery he counts it light
As to go clean himself from wound of brand,
And truly as you ride and go on land,
Though you had twenty lives to fling away,
May the knight hearken, you are overmanned.
The mischief he hath brewed!   Yet day by day
There's none can worst him, then by the great God I say,

E   65

Good Sir Gawayne, seek out some other track,
Whereso you will, and Christ be your good speed!
And look you now, for me, I will ride back
And swear you held right on with haste and heed.
By all the saints whom He found good indeed,
I shall keep faith, by God and by the Rood!
And tell no tale but prove true friend in need!"
"For thy good faith, friend, keep it I think thou would,
And may good luck be his who thinks to do me good.

Thou would'st be secret I believe it well,
But wert thou never so secret nor so fast,
I were not less a coward though none should tell:
Therefore go I.   Lo, how thou look'st aghast!
I say ere one hour be away and passed,
I will be there, though he were a stern knave,
As the fate drives so fare we at the last,
Though he be mighty and foul, armed with a stave,
Yet God can work full well his servants' lives to save."

"Marry, sith death thou'lt have, the road is clear,
Thou with thy talking have it thine own way,
I stay thee not but I'll not linger here;
Have now thy spear of me in rest to lay,
Thy helm eke: for the road 'tis as I say,
Boar-like he holds the bottom of this cleft,
Where he will tell a tale without delay
That thou shalt hearken; bear unto the left,
The clearing in the coombe.   Farewell of life bereft!

For here, Sir Knight, we twain part company,
I am no longer of thy fellowship
Though all the gold on earth should be my fee!"
He turns about and softly away doth slip
Threading the forest, and by holt and dip,
Strikes with his heels and left him all alone.
"By God's self," cries Gawayne, with steady lip,
"I am full ready, I will not weep nor groan,
Still will I look to God riding by stock and stone."

With that he strikes his heels into the steed,
And drives him downward deep into the dale
By the wild wood side, and at his topmost speed.
A savage place, he thought, the abode of bale.
Harbour he sees none yet, clearing, nor pale,
But knuckled crags of high and beetling stone
Which fill with menacing shadows all that vale;
On each side many a quick glance has he thrown
To spy his place of tryst, but Chapel sees he none.

Then he drew up his great steed at that tide,
And looked about and saw by his left hand,
Anigh a green bank by a river-side,
A round knoll in a clearing of the land,
That cunningly beside a ford was planned.
Here he lights down, full grim and hastily,
And fixed his bridle where the flung spray fanned
The rough boughs of a blackened linden-tree,
Debating doubtfully if that the place might be.

Nearer he draws to pass it and repass.
Much like a cave or crevice was that knoll,
And all about it grew the lank knot-grass.
Of size to admit a man there was an hole,
And all that place was hollow as a bowl.
"Is this the Chapel?" said the gentle knight,
"Yea God, at midnight when the skies are foul,
The Devil might tell his matins in good plight,
In such a waste as this with not much moon in sight.

Yea God, this oratory is ill-beseen,
All herb-o'ergrown so foully as it lies,
It falls but fit this fellow in the green
Should deal devotion here in devil-wise.
I feel it is the fiend who with his lies,
Hath lured me to this chapel of mischance,
This cursed kirk, to slay me in some guise,
Foul may it fall and low!" Then with high lance,
And helm whereon the frosty light doth play and glance,

E*   67

He strides thereto. Then loud o'er hill and plain
Rings out a sound, a wondrous and unblithe,
Grating as it should rend the cliff in twain,
Like, but for loudness thereof not a tithe,
As men upon a grindstone ground a scythe.
Louder it roars and rushes on the ear
Like waters at the mill that twist and writhe,
And, "by God," thinks Gawayne, "I trow that gear
Prepares for this same wizard who shall meet me here,

Yet the mere sound shall never terrify,
And so God's will be done," this is his gist,
And he advanced then, calling clear and high;
"With shield and spear and gauntlets to his wrist,
Here bides Gawayne, who waits to give him tryst?
Whoso seek aught, let him come hither fast;
Speak now: or never for his hour is missed!"
"Abide!" cries one from a high bank in that waste,
"Thou shalt have all I promised thee, and that in haste!"

Yet rapid for a space, with rush and whirr,
The whetting grateth, then he comes to light,
Fell from his hollow hill. He doth not stir,
Gawayne, but stone-still watches the green knight
Come by his crag, for a span broad and bright,
Within his right hand, worthy to be feared,
He bears of steel a Danish axe new-dight,
Which to a cunning edge the files have sheared;
Thus stands he with like looks, like locks, like bushy beard,

As when most strange he rode at Arthur's feast.
Only he lacks his steed, and his gaunt bones
He resteth on his axe, so on he pressed
And reaching where the water sobs and moans,
He bideth not to seek for stepping-stones,
But leaps it with his axe, no more but so.
"Thou can'st keep tryst!" and rattling to his tones
The echoes speak. Gawayne bows nothing low,
And on all sides about him lies the desolate snow.

"God keep thee, Gawayne, and God grant thee grace,
Thou holdest compact; cleanly it hath stood
This twelvemonth; welcome, warrior, to my place
Who time'st thy travel as a true man should.
Now are we two alone, and by my hood,
None like to part us in this valley deep;
Have off thy helm and sith few words are good,
Do of this thing no further comment keep
Than erst did I, when straightway and at one fell sweep,

This head of mine thou struck'st off and mad'st fall!"
—"By God who gave me a soul, even from my heart,
I grudge not nor refuse!   Whate'er befall,
Lo! I stand still: I neither stir nor start!
Dwell on the stroke; address thine axe with art!"
His semblance showing no whit of affright,
He bows, and for his neck, he shows that part
Bare to the naked flesh.   Then to an height
The other heaves his weapon with a great feint of might.

Him had he strucken, he had then left Gawayne
No better than the earth where he lay bleeding,
By such gross weight of metal cloven in twain,
But at its flash and at no other pleading,
He shrank a little, the load of steel receding
Sparkles the flints.   The other calls aloud;
"Lost to all worth, art thou then so unheeding
Of name and fame, Gawayne, the noble and proud?
Men said that never yet by no hill under cloud,

Nor any dale thou went'st aghast for fear,
And now he shakes before the buffet fall!
Who is this fellow? Never did I hear
Of Gawayne cowardice! Flinched I at all?
Did I raise tumults? No, in Arthur's hall,
This head of mine struck earth where all men stood!
Thus am I grown the greater, men shall call
Gawayne no more, 'the noble,' and 'the good'."
The knight cries; "I swerved once, but by the Holy Rood,

So will I now no more, wherefore apace!
Deal me the destiny for which I came
And bring me to the proof.   Here in thy place
I stand, abating nothing of thy claim;
But dream not thus to purchase greater fame,
For hark, if my head roll upon the plain,
Not being the Devil can I mend the same?"
"Have at thee then!" cries the other and amain
He heaves his axe as though to shiver bone and brain.

Yet even in striking he withholds the blow,
Staying it as it falls, that nothing boots.
Prepared, Gawayne abideth in the snow,
Fast as an oak-tree with an hundred roots,
Then hears he that gay voice which evilly suits
The grisly tenor of the speech; "Now like
Gawayne thou stand'st, and no man more imputes
Terror to thee, but yet thy hood up-pick,
Haply 'twill cover thy neck when I the buffet strike."

Then to him furiously returns Gawayne;
"Thrash on, bold warrior, thou who threaten'st long,
For now I deem it neither idle nor vain
To think thine heart but weak that was so strong
And never to be shook!"   "Therein thou art wrong,"
The other cries, "and have thy reckoning now!"
He gnaws his lip in knotting up the thong
Of blade and blade-shaft, puckering his deep brow;
He hath small need to love him he who beneath the bough,

Hopes for no rescue.   Now the man in green
Lightly heaves up his huge axe to an height:
Yet all as lightly lets it fall agen!
It seemed he would have hammered with all his might,
Yet did the steel into the flesh not bite
But graze the neck: sever the skin thereon;
A spear's length and a span, prepared to fight,
Gawayne leaps back; he knows the compact done,
Seeing there, on the bright snow, the bloody drops that shone!

So joyous: his like the world can scarce afford!
His broad shield from his shoulders where it lay,
He jerks before him; flourishes his bright sword,
And cries in arms, "Bid no more blows to-day!
One single stroke, as no man will gainsay,
Concludes the compact, erewhile shaped right so;
Then for a blow a blow I will repay,
And (trust me) fiercely, speak then, ay or no,
If thou resist or fighting tender blow for blow?"

Herewith the green knight holding back a space,
His perilous axe-haft leant unto the ground,
Looks upon Gawayne, how within that place
Dreadless he stands in arms and safe and sound—
Armed head to heel—Sir Gawayne the renowned.
The other liked that; bellowing boisterously,
(His voice a very tempest of deep sound)
"Wherefore so fierce of face, Knight?" crieth he,
"There is no man on earth that hath mishandled thee,

Nor done aught mannerless, but only so
As at King's court and worthily was shaped.
I promised and I proffered thee a blow,
And thou hast had it, happy having scaped
All claims beside; if twice I feigned and japed,
Yet the third time, I might in honesty,
Have strucken thee a blow that wider gaped,
For twice erewhile thou dealed'st faithfully,
But the third time what then? Thou can'st it not deny,

It is my weed thou hast about thy waist,
A girdle woven of my lady's woof.
My trust in thee not evilly was placed
The first time and the second, and the proof,
Those kisses given beneath my castle roof,
When I returned from hunting where I rode;
But on the third night to your own behoof,
You kept back half, that girdle that you owed,
And on a compact broken quitted my abode.

71

For those two nights, I feinted, without scathe,
And for the third night thou hast had thy pay;
'When true man truly gives,' the proverb saith,
'No ill to him befalls.'   I know, I say,
The converse and the kisses of each day,
My lady's wooing also, never doubt—
Small wonder, for I wrought it every way—
I might have wrought you mischief at this bout,
But count all claims against you as clean cancelled out.

I sent her to assay thee and I find
Thou art the rose of princes without peer,
For so thou dost excel unto my mind
All knights beside, as truly fair and clear,
A princely pearl that had by chance come there
With white peas in a bushel, more delights
Than they, and doth more lustrously appear,
(Men count it for a trove in their despites)
So doth the gay Gawayne excel all earthly knights.

But here a little you lacked for loyalty,
But sith for love of life the less your blame;
Had it been amorous work wrought covertly
By wooing my wife, 'twere slaughter to your fame;
But unassailed my lady went and came,
Her gift a charm, no love-gift last or first."
But Gawayne hears not, only in his hot shame,
Even to his yellow hair the red blood burst,
"Be avarice," he cries, "and be thou, cowardice, accursed,

In you is vice that virtue doth betray,
And villany!"   He thrusteth in his hand
And from his body plucks the lace away,
And casts it to that Lord on snowy land.
"This thing is with my sorrows wrought and planned,
This wizardry bade fear with avarice
Conspire to thrust me from that glorious band
That generous freedom love and count it bliss,
And loyalty—judge then what wealth I have in this.

Oh, treachery and untruth, through you come sorrow,
And bitter grief to men and biting care,
And though we walk more warely on the morrow,
This grief is ours to-day!" His deep despair
The green man breaks through with a merrier air,
"Confession," quoth he, "putteth all to rights,
And what hurt have I? Truly I am bare
Of any. Take this girdle of delights,
A keepsake from the encounter of two chivalrous knights!

I hold thee utterly confessed and clean,
Have then my girdle with its hasps of gold,
Look on its hue, the brightest ever seen,
As green as ever my gown, and then be bold
By this to mind a story long since told,
When you ride forth with captains of the best,
Of this same Chapel by the waters cold.
And sith as now but little time doth rest,
Revel away with me the remnant of this feast.

With your old enemy," laughing loud he cries,
"Accord you, come, you're welcome I you tell!"
"May He reward you fair," Gawayne replies,
"That is the Ruler both of dale and fell.
For me I sojourn sadly by your dell,
And tarry but unhappy by your hall,
Commend me to mine honoured lady well,
And to mine other honoured ladies all,
That with their sleights so cunningly their guest made fall.

Fool that I was! But though far less than those,
The great of old time, tricked with woman's wile,
With them I stand; Adam in garden-close,
And David whom Barsabe led with guile,
And Samson, whom she overreached a mile
Who shore his locks, he may awaken loath!
And Solomon the King, whom they erewhile
So wasted that his wisdom slept in sloth—
God, that man might at once both love and distrust both!

Those four were fooled, the highest under Heaven,
By witchery of women that they used,
Shorn of the glory that of God was given,
And with high things to mind, on them they mused;
Be mine with their faults pardoned and excused;
But for your girdle, give me that again,
Nor marvel much that I before refused
And now accept it—not for the bright green stain,
Silk-work nor joy of gold, but for to be my bane,

That with this gay-wrought girdle at my side,
In gorgeous company when I ride forth,
—Lifted above the world in joy and pride—
Seeing this I may reflect; 'In death and birth,
Ay, all life through, how slight is man of worth,
And to unchastity how ready and weak.'
Thus in the triumph of joy and sorrow's dearth,
I may depress my heart one look to seek
Of this green girdle.   One thing further let me speak:

Your name?   therefore I demand no more."
The other answers, "Truly as I guess,
Bernlak Hautdesert am I upon this shore,
Through might of Morgan, erst Merlin's mistréss—
Morgan the fairy, Morgan the goddéss—
'Tis she that lives within my house hereby,
In craft deep learn'd and wiles of bookishness
That clerks of old time writ full cunningly.
There is no knight on earth so noble nor so high

But she can tame him and his power despise.
With that wise Merlin who knew well your knights
She lived of old in passing loving wise,
And he, in quaintness of his clerkly sleights,
To keep her love would show her magic rites,
And all charms show her to delight her ear.
She sent me to your high hall of delights
To bring to her report if truth it were
The Table's greatness; further, hating Guinevere,

The sleights she taught me of that ghostly speaker
Holding his own head your high table by,
In malice, upon Guinevere to wreak her
Fury; in hopes she might from terror die!
She is that ancient lady verily;
Her noble race doth from Tintagel spring—
The Duchess' daughter of that town is she—
Deep versed in craft, she did my young wife bring
To trick thee with the love-lace.   Uther whom they sing,

The poets, Uther got erst by that dame,
Arthur that very king and lord is now
This Britain through.   Return then, slough thy shame,
Come, Warrior, to thine aunt—thou wilt, I trow,
For my folk love thee, no man more, and thou—"
But Gawayne answers; "Never in no wise."
Therefore they part for ever under bough,
Each kissing each, by snow and steely ice,
And each commending each to Christ and Paradise.

O'er wild ways of the world rideth Gawayne,
Grace gotten of his life, with horse and mail,
Sheltered ofttimes, oft camped in open plain,
Beneath the stars adventuring by vale,
Whereof if any list to shape the tale,
There is much matter.   Me, I say but this,
To court he comes at last, a knight all hale,
And Queen and King there greet him with a kiss,
And all men wake anew to fellowship in bliss.

They ask him of his travels, all doth he tell,
Joys and a many sorrows overpassed,
His banqueting, his chance at Green Chapél,
The lady's love and love-lace at the last:
From his white neck the yellow locks he cast,
And shows the brand of his untruth for blame,
To his fair face the red blood flies and fast,
And all his spirits pure sorrow overcame;
"Lo, lord," he cries, "the lace, of my illhap and shame!

I swore to bear this brand of cowardice
In all men's sights, the symbol of my heart.
Let no man hide his hurt for truth it is,
Who stoops to fault from fault he may not start
And deeds ill done time cures nor no man's art."
But all those knights a green-wrought baldrick bound
Bright on their breasts, to blaze in every part,
Whereso i' th' world they voyaged over ground,
The token of the honour of the Table-Round,

Even all King Arthur's knights by south and north,
A sign of highest honour ever more,
As in the Brutus Books it is set forth,
(Cited in tale my witnesses before,
That he was honoured that the green lace bore)
Sith Brutus with a new-awakening joy,
Held on toward these white cliffs and rocky shore,
O'er the wide waters' turbulent annoy,
When siege and shock of battle broke the antique Troy.

I-wis,
Adventures many enow
Have fallen before ere this:
But He with the Thorn on Brow,
May He bring all to Bliss.   Amen.

HONY SOYT QUI MAL PENCE.

NOTES

Second Personal Pronoun. Old English used the singular only in addressing one person, but in the Middle English of the fourteenth century *ye* was also used, but in special circumstances. Skeat thus summarises: "*Thou* is the language of a lord to a servant, of an equal to an equal, and expresses also companionship, love, permission, defiance, scorn, and threatening. . . . *Ye* is the language of a servant to a lord, and of compliment, and further expresses honour, submission, entreaty." Jespersen says: "The distinction between the two forms of addressing one person corresponds pretty nearly to that of the French *tu* and *vous*, but it was looser, as very frequently one person addressed the same other person now with *thou*, now with *you* (*ye*), according as the tone of the conversation changed ever so slightly." The use of the second form of address in *Sir Gawayne* is very subtle and interesting, and adds much to the dramatic force of many passages; the mixed use should be studied with especial care; the translator has reproduced exactly the use of the original.

16. ii. 9. Or perhaps "under Christ himself, *i.e.* under the rule of Christ."

17. iv. 7-9. To be strictly accurate the seating at the high-table appears to have been as follows:—

Agravayne. Gawayne. Guinevere. Arthur. Bawdwin. Ywain.

28. ii. 6. This is the translation if the MS. reading be retained, but MS. *sage* may be a mistake for *fage*, in which case the general sense would be, "as the general scheme of things (the world) certainly demands."

32. ii. 3-4. The geography is vague, but it appears to be quite certain that this cannot be the Holyhead in Anglesey. Such an identification would appear to be ruled out by the line, *Alle ꝑe iles of Anglesay on lyft half he haldeʒ.* Presumably some place is meant, which is no longer called by that name, where Gawayne crossed the Dee into Wirral. Various suggested identifications have been made, but evidence in favour of any of them is lacking.

35. iii. 9. Whilst *fre of hys speche*, in the modern sense of "free," would suit the context here, the more so as it gives the Green Knight's characteristic of generosity, it should be borne in mind that *fre* in the sense of "noble"—OE. *freo*—is very commonly found in Middle English. Either sense may be intended here.

43. ii. 7. The translation here follows the practice of earlier editors in taking the MS. *abloi* to be an interjection from OFr. *ablo*. More recent editors, however, prefer derivation from OFr. *esbloi* "reckless, transported with delight," in which case the sense would be, "the lord, carried away with joy, often rode forth and alighted."

45. iv. 8-9. This passage is ambiguous in the original, but the meaning appears to be, ". . . for I have found in you a noble generosity. Others receive much from other people according to their deeds; but the favour that I receive is not because of any merit on my part. The honour that you show me is simply because of the generosity of one who can only behave with courtesy." Gawayne tells the lady that her generosity leads her to believe him a nobler man than he is.

49. iii. 7-9. *ker* is taken here as from OE. *carr* "stone, rock," but the form of the word suggests rather derivation from ON. *kjarr* "marsh." "They uncoupled the hounds which ran questing through the thorn bushes. Soon they call for a search to be made at the side of a marsh, and the huntsman encourages the hounds that first give tongue."

53. iii. This account of the unlacing of the boar, which might prove distasteful to modern readers, has been condensed into a single stanza. The four lines there omitted are appended here for the sake of completeness. Literally the passage runs: "After (the having off of the head) he breaks out the bowels, broils them on the ashes, and rewards his hounds with bread blent therewith. Then he breaks out the brawn in bright, broad, shields and, as fitly beseems, has the haslets out; and yet fastens them all whole, the halves together."

56. ii. 1. This is the translation of the text as punctuated by some editors. C. Brett, however (*Modern Language Review*, viii. 163), suggests that the MS. should be read as *mydouervnder* rather than *myd ouer vnder*. This would mean that the fox eluded the hunting party until about ten-thirty a.m. if we suppose *undern* to have here its usual and earlier meaning of nine in the morning.

56. iii. 3. A difficult passage in the original. The translation given here presupposes that the MS. *hweʒ goud* is a scribal error for some such phrase as *heue gold* "heavy gold," and a contrast would then be intended between the heaviness of the metal and the lightness of the gems. It seems likely enough that we have to do with a copyist's error here, though as it stands the manuscript could perhaps be translated, "No bright colours on her head except for well-wrought gems."

57. i. 7-9. This is the translation of the actual manuscript reading, but modern editors usually take *mare*, in the line *Nif mare of hir knyʒt mynne*, to be a mistake for *Marye*. In that case the sense would be, "Danger is nigh to them unless St. Mary have thought for her knight, *i.e.* for Gawayne."

65. iv. 7. An ambiguous passage. If *the knight* refers to Gawayne then the translation is as above, but perhaps it refers to the *Green Knight*, and the sense then would be, "If you come there you will be killed if the Green Knight have his way."

74. iii. 3. The name of the Green Knight was printed as *Bernlak* by earlier editors of the romance, but a re-examination of the manuscript by later editors has made it clear that what was read as n is really *ci*, or perhaps *ti*. Hence his name should read *Bercilak*, or *Bertilak, de Hautdesert*.

APPENDIX

The following is transcribed from the photographic facsimile of the manuscript edited by Sir Israel Gollancz for the Early English Text Society, and thanks are due to the Society for permission to print it. The manuscript reading is retained throughout, but the punctuation and capitalization have been modernized. This extract should be compared with page 64, stanza ii, to page 65, stanza iii, of the translation above.

> Thenne watȝ Gryngolet graype, þat gret watȝ & huge,
> & hade ben soiourned sauerly & in a siker wyse,
> Hym lyst prik for poynt, þat proude hors þenne;
> Þe wyȝe wynneȝ hym to, & wyteȝ on his lyre,
> & sayde soberly hym-self & by his soth swereȝ,
> "Here is a meyny in þis mote þat on menske þenkkeȝ;
> Þe mon hem maynteines, ioy mot þay haue!
> Þe leue lady on lyue, luf hir bityde!
> Ȝif þay for charyte cherysen a gest,
> & halden honour in her honde; þe haþel hem ȝelde
> Þat haldeȝ þe heuen vpon hyȝe, & also yow alle!
> & ȝif I myȝt lyf vpon londe lede any quyle,
> I schuld rech yow sum rewarde redyly, if I myȝt."
> Þenn steppeȝ he in-to stirop & strydeȝ alofte;
> His schalk schewed hym his schelde, on schulder he hit laȝt,
> Gordeȝ to Gryngolet with his gilt heleȝ,
> & he starteȝ on þe ston, stod he no lenger
>   to praunce;
>   His haþel on hors watȝ þenne,
>   Þat bere his spere & launce.
>   "Þis kastel to Kryst I kenne,
>   He gef hit ay god chaunce!"

> The brygge watȝ brayde doun, & þe brode ȝateȝ
> Vnbarred & born open vpon boþe halue;
> Þe burne blessed hym bilyue, & þe bredeȝ passed;
> Prayses þe porter, bifore þe prynce kneled,
> Gef hym God & goud day, þat Gawayn he saue;
> & went on his way with his wyȝe one
> Þat schulde teche hym to tourne to þat tene place
> Þer þe ruful race he schulde re-sayue.

Þay boȝen bi bonkkeȝ þer boȝeȝ ar bare,
Þay clomben bi clyffeȝ þer clengeȝ þe colde;
Þe heuen watȝ vp-halt, bot vgly þer-vnder
Mist muged on þe mor, malt on þe mounteȝ;
Vch hille hade a hatte, a myst-hakel huge;
Brokeȝ byled & breke bi bonkkeȝ aboute,
Schyre schaterande on schoreȝ, þer þay doun schowued.
Welawylle watȝ þe way þer þay bi wod schulden,
Til hit watȝ sone sesoun þat þe sunne ryses
           þat tyde;
     Þay were on a hille ful hyȝe,
     Þe quyte snaw lay bisyde;
     Þe burne þat rod hym by
     Bede his mayster abide.

"For I haf wonnen yow hider, wyȝe, at þis tyme,
& now nar ȝe not fer fro þat note place
Þat ȝe han spied & spuryed so specially after;
Bot I schal say yow forsoþe, syþen I yow knowe,
& ȝe ar a lede vpon lyue þat I wel louy,
Wolde ȝe worch bi my wytte, ȝe worþed þe better.
Þe place þat ȝe prece to ful perelous is halden;
Þer woneȝ a wyȝe in þat waste, þe worste vpon erþe;
For he is stiffe & sturne, & to strike louies,
& more he is þen any mon vpon myddelerde,
& his body bigger þen þe best fowre
Þat ar in Arthureȝ hous, Hestor oþer oþer."

SELECT BIBLIOGRAPHY

Facsimile of the Middle English Text.

Facsimile Reproduction of Cotton Nero A. x. Introduction by Sir
I. Gollancz (Early English Text Society, No. 162: London,
1923).

Editions of the Middle English Text.

F. Madden, *Syr Gawayne* (Bannatyne Club, 1839).

R. Morris, *Sir Gawayne and The Green Knight* (Early English Text
Society, No. 4: London, 1864; revised by the author, 1869,
by Sir I. Gollancz, 1897).

J. R. R. Tolkien and E. V. Gordon, *Sir Gawain and The Green
Knight* (Oxford University Press, 1925).

Sir I. Gollancz and M. Day, *Sir Gawain and The Green Knight* (Early
English Text Society, No. 210: London, 1940).

Edition of Poems by the same Author.

C. S. Osgood, *The Pearl* (Belles-Lettres Series: Boston and
London, 1906).

Sir I. Gollancz, *Patience* (London, 1913).

R. J. Menner, *Purity* (Yale Studies in English, lxi.: Yale University
Press, 1920).

Sir I. Gollancz, *St. Erkenwald* (London, 1922).

Modernizations of Sir Gawain and the Green Knight.

Jessie L. Weston, *Sir Gawain and the Green Knight* (London,
1898).

J. H. Cox, *Knighthood in Germ and Flower* (Boston, 1910), pp. 93-
187.

E. J. B. Kirtlan, *Sir Gawain and the Green Knight* (London, 1912).

Jessie L. Weston, *Romance, Vision and Satire* (London, 1912).

W. A. Neilson and K. G. T. Webster, *Chief British Poets of the
Fourteenth and Fifteenth Centuries* (Boston, 1916), pp. 21-47.

K. Hare, *Sir Gawayne and the Green Knight* (Stratford, 1918).

H. A. Watt and J. B. Munn, *Ideas and Forms in English and American
Literature* (New York, 1925).

T. H. Banks, *Sir Gawain and the Green Knight* (New York,
1929).

S. O. Andrew, *Sir Gawain and the Green Knight* (London, 1929).

G. H. Gerould, *Beowulf and Sir Gawain* (New York, 1934).

G. H. Gerould, *Beowulf to Shakespeare* (New York, 1938), part i., pp. 132-199.

Sources.

Jessie L. Weston, *The Legend of Sir Gawain* (Grimm Library, No. vii.: London, 1897).

G. Henderson, *Fled Bricrend* (Irish Texts Society, No. ii.: London, 1899).

G. L. Kittredge, *A Study of Gawain and the Green Knight* (Harvard University Press, 1916).

E. K. Chambers, *Arthur of Britain* (London, 1927).

R. S. Loomis, *Celtic Myth and Arthurian Romance* (Columbia University Press, 1927).

Medieval Hunting Treatises.

Sir H. Dryden, *The Art of Hunting* (1843); re-edited by Alice Dryden (Northampton, 1908). Contains *Le Art de Venerie* by Guyllame Twici, huntsman to Edward II; a fifteenth-century English translation of Twici's work entitled *The Craft of Venery*; and a translation of a thirteenth-century French poem, *La Chase dou Cerf.*

W. A. Baillie-Grohman, *The Master of Game* (London, 1904, 2nd ed. 1909). The earliest treatise in English on the subject. Written by Edward, 2nd Duke of York, probably between 1406 and 1413.

Dame Juliana Berners (Barnes?), *The Boke of St. Albans* (St. Albans, 1486). Re-edited in facsimile by W. Blades (London, n.d.). Contains treatises on Hunting, Hawking, and Coat Armour traditionally ascribed to Juliana Berners (Barnes?), prioress of Sopwell.

G. Turbervile, *The Noble Art of Venerie or Hunting* (London, 1576). Reprinted in the Tudor and Stuart Library, 1908. A translation of *La Venerie* by Jacques Du Fouilloux, printed at Rouen in 1561.

See also:—

H. L. Savage, "Hunting in the Middle Ages" (*Speculum*, viii. 30-41).

H. L. Savage, "The Significance of the Hunting Scenes in *Sir Gawain and the Green Knight*" (*Journal of English and Germanic Philology*, xxvii. 1-15).

Similar descriptions of hunting are found also in the two following Middle English romances:—

G. P. McNeill, *Sir Tristrem* (Scottish Text Society, 1886).

Sir I. Gollancz, *The Parlement of the Three Ages* (London, 1915).

Medieval Costume.

J. R. Planché, *A Cyclopaedia of Costume* (London, 1876), 2 vols.

H. W. Macklin, *The Brasses of England* (London, 1907; 3rd ed. 1913).

H. Druitt, *Manual of Costume as Illustrated by Monumental Brasses* (London, 1906).

M. and C. H. B. Quennell, *A History of Everyday Things in England* (London, 1918-34), 4 vols., Vol. i, 1066-1499.

M. G. Houston, *Medieval Costume in England and France* (London, 1939).

Castle Architecture.

A. Hamilton Thompson, *Military Architecture in England during the Middle Ages* (Oxford University Press, 1912).

Language and Metre of the Poem.

J. P. Oakden, *Alliterative Poetry in Middle English* (Manchester University Press, 1930-35). 2 vols.

Literary Aspects.

The Cambridge History of English Literature, i. 243 ff., 320 ff.

F. J. Snell, *The Age of Chaucer* (London, 1899).

W. H. Schofield, *English Literature from the Norman Conquest to Chaucer* (London, 1906).

W. P. Ker, *English Literature, Medieval* (London, 1912).

A. B. Taylor, *An Introduction to Medieval Romance* (London, 1930).

G. Sampson, *The Concise Cambridge History of English Literature* (London, 1941).

Bibliographical.

A full account of all books and articles on the subject will be found in J. E. Wells, *A Manual of the Writings in Middle English, 1050-1400*. With *Supplements I-VIII* (Yale University Press: London, 1916-41).